HEROES
OF THE NEW AGE

We (must) strive to remodel our lives
after the pattern of sublime heroism associated
with those gone before us.

Shoghi Effendi

HEROES
OF THE NEW AGE

by

Edward Nadeau Diliberto

GEORGE RONALD PUBLISHER

OXFORD

George Ronald, *Publisher*
Oxford
www.grbooks.com

*A catalogue record for this book is available
from the British Library*

ISBN 978–0–85398–576–1

Cover design: Steiner Graphics

CONTENTS

I dedicate this to my wife,
Evelyn Mae Diliberto,
and our seven children

INTRODUCTION

It is difficult for the reader to fully appreciate the thrilling deeds of the heroes told about in this book without some knowledge of the condition of Persia at the time these events took place, so many years ago.

Everyone who has studied that period of history reports that Persia was a backward nation, sunk in a sea of cruelty, narrow-mindedness and dishonesty. This was all the more sad and tragic because this condition was so different from how it had been in ancient times; in those olden days Persia was famous for its arts, culture, government, cities and riches.

At the time the Báb declared His mission in 1844, the country was in the iron grip of the Shah, the king of that land. Since the people had no voice in the government, he could do exactly as he pleased. He and he alone had the power of life or death over every person in his kingdom. Punishments and death sentences were his way of making people obey him; and these were carried out in the most brutal manner imaginable. Anyone who appeared to present the slightest threat to his authority would be destroyed.

It was impossible for the Shah to be fair to his people even if he desired to do so. Most of the officials who

1

served him were selfish and dishonest and cared nothing for the good of the people of the land. They were only interested in making themselves as rich as possible while in office. An official would bring a matter to the Shah only when he had been secretly paid to do so, or he was seeking a special favour for himself. For this reason the Shah could never get to the facts of a matter and was kept in the dark as to the true state of affairs in his country; so his people remained in misery.

The state of religion in Persia was no better. A cruel and close-minded Muslim clergy, working hand in hand with the government, controlled every detail of the social life of the people, and taught them to hate anyone who believed differently from them. The people were kept in ignorance and forced to follow without question whatever the mullas demanded of them. Weighed down with such a cruel government and ungodly religious system, the people were easily moved toward cruelty, intolerance and bloodthirstiness.

Because of these conditions, the Báb must have known the kind of reception He would receive at the hands of His countrymen. But He did not allow any such thought to hold Him back from His mission, nor did it hold back the band of His early followers from withstanding every hardship along the path of their new-found Faith. The fact that the Báb was bringing a new religion meant that all the cruelty of the religious and governmental leaders would have to end. These leaders were especially afraid that if this new religion spread among the people they would lose their control over them. And so from the beginning they were against the Báb and tried to defeat Him by any means possible.

With this background information in mind, let us begin our story by recounting one of the most stirring events of those thrilling days of yester-year, an event that boldly demonstrated the character of those men and women who took up the Cause of the Báb, the Heroes of the New Age.

CHAPTER ONE

A DARK WINTER'S NIGHT

The date was 2 February 1849. The setting was a forested area in the northern part of Persia. Blackness filled the night. Snow covered the ground. Frost chilled the air. A band of innocent men had taken refuge in a small building where a holy man was buried. To protect themselves against attack they built log walls all around it, turning it into a fort. They were surrounded on all sides by an army sent by the government with orders to destroy them to the last man. The soldiers had constructed a series of barricades in front of the fort; each barricade was under the command of an officer and his squad of soldiers. A good distance behind these barricades the army officers' tents were set up. From these positions the army had launched attack after attack against the little fort. The men inside had suffered many casualties, and their food and supplies had nearly run out. In spite of this suffering and starvation they remained strong, and their spirits high, for they were struggling for the freedom of their Faith.

All was quiet along the army lines as the sleepy soldiers settled in for a cold, dark winter's night. Not so with the oppressed band of defenders behind the walls they had built; all were alert and ready for action, their eyes fixed upon the man in their midst who was the most valiant

4

warrior among them. He was more awake than he had ever been in his life – every nerve of his body was surging with energy, he was ready for action. They watched and listened to him as he strode to and fro, inspiring them with words of encouragement. The battles had diminished neither his courage nor his energy. He was dressed entirely in white, and he wore a green turban on his head. A great sword rested in its scabbard at his side. His small stature, lean build and frail appearance gave little clue to the strength and agility he possessed. A short beard set off the keen, bright look of his face. He was in the prime of his life.

Earlier in the afternoon, during a lull in the battle, a forethought of what was going to happen to him entered his mind. He knew that the end of his life was near, and that now was the time to make his supreme, last effort in the defence of his Faith. As he paced back and forth a plan began to form in his mind. Suddenly he stopped and turned to his companions, who had been watching his every move. Calmly, he explained to them what he planned to do. They would wait until after midnight when the soldiers would be asleep, charge out from the fort in the pitch of darkness, and, catching the enemy by surprise, strike their final blow for liberty. They all accepted his invitation to join him in this bold move. Gathering together the few weapons they had, he got them ready for battle; some would be on horseback and others would follow on foot. He would lead the charge. Everyone was in their place waiting for his command. He was satisfied that all was ready and his moment of destiny had arrived.

The freezing early morning air suddenly came to

life. The warrior leaped upon his charger, and with the most encouraging words rallied the spirit of his men. Unsheathing his sword, he wheeled his mount about and gave the order to open the log gates of their simple fort. The big horse pranced and flared its nostrils, sensing the air of battle. Raising a war-cry that echoed from one end of the forest to the other, he spurred his mount into full gallop and charged out of the gates, his men following fast behind him. Shattering the cold of the night, the thundering hooves of his stallion picked up speed as he directed his horse straight at the enemy. The rush of his attack in the frosty darkness came like the blast of a hot wind across the stretch of ground between the fort and the enemy lines. The cold and sleepy soldiers behind the first barricade were caught by complete surprise; frozen with fear, they did not know where to turn. His great horse carrying him over the first barricade, the valiant warrior cut down its commander and scattered his terrified men. Forward he dashed, the searing heat of his charge melting away all resistance before him. Onward he stormed, overcoming every barricade that stood in his way. Pounding hooves and flashing sword – not a single soldier had the courage to stand and face him! So powerful was the driving force of his charge that it carried him all the way to the officers' tents beyond the barricades. His companions following in hot pursuit, they roared through the enemy camp like a tornado, trampling everything under the horses' hooves, upsetting tables and lamps, knocking over tents and men, dealing out the punishment the oppressors so justly deserved.

Those officers and soldiers who escaped the wrath of that inspired warrior and his men scrambled for cover. A rifleman reached a tree, climbed it, and hid in its branches. From this safe perch he lay in wait to get a shot at the dauntless band. As he watched, a fire suddenly broke out and quickly spread in every direction. The flames only added to the confusion of the scene. In the blinding glare of the burning camp, and with the rifleman in the tree watching, the horse of the valiant leader became entangled in the ropes of a tent. This delayed him just long enough for the rifleman to take careful aim at him and fire. The bullet struck the hero in the chest. Down he fell from his horse. Blood pouring from his wound, he staggered a few steps and fell to the ground.

Imagine the awe-inspiring sight! The frothing warhorses lathered with sweat, the ringing clash of steel upon steel, the sound of gunfire and bullets whizzing through the air, the pitiful groans of dying men littering the ground, the whole dreadful scene illuminated by the reddish flames of the raging fire, and the heroic warrior fallen to the ground. The name of this man was Mullá Ḥusayn.

To understand the circumstances that led to this dramatic scene, we must go back in time, to more than four years before, to 22 May 1844. That was the day the spiritual forces that led to this stirring event were set loose. These same forces would account for the other remarkable tales that adorn the pages of this story, and, in time, attain such a magnitude that the direction of the history of the world would be changed forever.

CHAPTER TWO

A NEW PROPHET IS IN THE WORLD

The day of 22 May 1844 opened the most glorious Age in the spiritual history of mankind. On that day the spectacular story of the Master Hero, the Báb, began. On this day the Báb initiated a divine revelation that was to shake the very foundations of the land of its birth, Persia, and eventually reach every corner of the globe. The purifying force of its light would call forth a band of souls of matchless spiritual strength and heroism; repelled by this same light, the forces of darkness would rear their ugly heads and reveal the depths of human wickedness.

The first to appear in this drama was the young man Mullá Ḥusayn, the fate of whom you have just learned. After a period of long study of the Holy Books and intense prayer and meditation, he had become convinced that the time had come for God to reveal to mankind His new Messenger. The desire to find this Messenger grew so strong in him that he made it the whole purpose of his life. Every wakeful thought, every sleepful dream was filled with visions of how he might discover God's Manifestation in his own day. For forty days he prayed and fasted in order to prepare himself for his mission to find

Him, and when these days ended he was ready. Leaving everything behind, and relying on trust in God as the best provision for his journey, he set out on foot towards the South. Crossing mountains and traversing deserts, he pushed onward on his holy quest. Enduring hunger, thirst, cold and hardship, he pushed onward, nothing could hold him back. Although he did not know it at the time, the Divine Hand was guiding him every step of the way, for he had been chosen by the Báb to be the first to hear the call of God and believe it.

Onward he trudged, moving irresistibly towards the southern region of Persia. At last he arrived before the gate to the city of Shiraz. Still unaware of the Hand that guided him, his eye caught sight of the Báb standing by the side of the gate as he approached. It looked as though He was waiting for someone. A brilliant light suddenly seemed to shine from Him, startling Mullá Ḥusayn for a moment. The Báb walked straight to him and welcomed him with loving-kindness as if he were an old friend. Although Mullá Ḥusayn had seen Him before, nevertheless he was quite surprised by this warm greeting.

Although somewhat overcome by this unexpected welcome, yet he felt at ease because of the friendliness, charm and regal manner of the Báb. He still had no thought that he had found the One for whom he had been looking. The Báb invited him to visit His home, which was not far from where they stood, and he accepted this invitation without hesitation. Arriving there shortly, the Báb led him inside and treated him with the greatest kindness and hospitality imaginable. In time their conversation led to the subject of Mullá Ḥusayn's mission. He explained to the Báb that he was convinced that God's new Messenger was on earth and that for countless days he had been searching to find Him. In the course of their conversation the Báb was gradually awakening him to the fact that He was the very Messenger for Whom he searched. Finally, this realization began to sink into the heart and mind of Mullá Ḥusayn.

As the night wore on, the time for which Mullá Ḥusayn had been destined to witness began to approach; the time for the declaration of the Promised One of God to mankind! Little by little the fact that he had reached his goal, that he was in the presence of God's Messenger to mankind, began to penetrate his soul. Every part of him, body and soul, began to respond to what was happening. A cold sweat broke out on his brow, his hands and feet began to shake. Then, lightning-like, the shock of recognition struck: the voice of the Báb was the voice of God Himself! He felt faint as he realized he had found the object of his quest!

All that happened that night is not known, but the remarks left by Mullá Ḥusayn about that moment indicate how he must have swooned away with the ecstasy and joy of that meeting. This is his account: 'This Revelation . . . came as a thunderbolt which, for a time, seemed to have benumbed my faculties. I was blinded by its dazzling splendour and overwhelmed by its crushing force. Excitement, joy, awe, and wonder stirred the depths of my soul.'

On and on they talked until the break of dawn. As the

rays of the new day's sun spread across the city, these words were spoken by the Báb to Mullá Ḥusayn:

'O thou who art the first to believe in me! Verily I say, I am the Báb, the Gate of God, and thou art . . . the gate of that Gate. Eighteen souls must . . . accept Me and recognize the truth of My Revelation . . . we shall appoint unto each of the eighteen souls his special mission, and shall send them forth to accomplish their task. We shall instruct them to teach the Word of God and to quicken the souls of men.'

And so it happened that Mullá Ḥusayn found the Desire of his heart, and came to be the first to believe in the great Cause of God. By doing so he set his course to become a matchless champion and hero of the Cause of the Báb. One by one eighteen souls did accept and believe in the Báb, just as He foretold they would. And each one dedicated his entire life to His Cause.

These first eighteen believers were given a unique title by the Báb; each was to be known as a 'Letter of the Living'. Besides Mullá Ḥusayn, two other Letters of the Living are of special importance. These are Quddús and Ṭáhirih.

Ṭáhirih was a beautiful young woman known for her passion for religious truth. She came to believe in the Báb by contact through the spiritual world. One night she saw the face of the Báb in a dream, and soon after sent a message for Him that said, 'The effulgence of Thy face flashed forth . . . Then speak the word, "Am I not your Lord?" and "Thou art, Thou art!" we will all reply.' She became one of the chief disciples of the Báb. She was to

11

be martyred in the most horrible manner because of her new-found faith. You will learn more of her story later.

A young handsome man of twenty-two years of age, named Quddús, was also certain that the time was at hand for God to reveal to mankind a new Messenger. Like the Báb, he was a descendant of the Prophet Muhammad and therefore shown the respect due to that sacred lineage. He had been praying with all his heart that God would lead him to this Messenger. Then it happened. Like Ṭáhirih, he came to discover the Báb by way of the spiritual world. One evening he was walking along the same street in the town of Shiraz as were the Báb and Mullá Ḥusayn. Quddús approached them, and at first sight of the Báb he recognized that He could be none other than the true Promised One whom he had been so earnestly seeking.

Mullá Ḥusayn tried to calm him, but Quddús gave him no heed, saying, 'Why seek you to hide Him from me? I can recognize Him by His gait. I confidently testify that none besides Him . . . can claim to be the Truth. None other can manifest the power and majesty that radiate from His holy person.'

Mullá Ḥusayn was amazed upon hearing these words from Quddús.

'Marvel not,' said the Báb. 'We have in the world of spirit been communing with that youth. We know him already. We indeed awaited his coming.'

This shows that even though they may be distant in body, the heroes of God are always in contact with their Lord. Though young in age, Quddús was to show a degree of courage and spiritual leadership no other disciple of the Báb would exceed. Soon you shall read in this book of his great adventures.

With the enlistment of Quddús among the Letters of the Living, the number of eighteen prescribed by the Báb was complete. The next task would be to assign to each of them a special mission to spread the new Word of God.

CHAPTER THREE

THE CALL IS SENT FORTH

When the Báb told the purpose of His mission to Mullá Ḥusayn that memorable night, a divinely propelled process was set into motion, a process that would be world-transforming in its ultimate consequences.

To add momentum to this process, the Báb decided to spread the news across the land that He, the Promised One of God, was in the world. First He asked to see one of the Letters of the Living, Mullá 'Alí. With the following words He sent him on his teaching mission:

'Your faith must be as immovable as the rock, must weather every storm and survive every calamity . . . For you are called to partake of the celestial banquet prepared for you in the immortal Realm. You are the first to leave the House of God, and to suffer for His sake.'

No sooner had Mullá 'Alí set out on his mission than an extraordinary event took place. A young shopkeeper in the town had a very vivid dream. In his dream he saw and heard a town crier announce in the streets of his town the appearance of a most Holy Man distributing 'charters of liberty' to the people, and that the blessings of Paradise would descend upon anyone who received them! The next morning when he came upon Mullá 'Alí in the street, he could hardly believe his eyes – he was the very town crier of his dream! He approached him and told him of his dream, and how he was the very man in the dream distributing charters of liberty to the people! On the spot, he passionately declared his desire to follow Mullá 'Alí on his journey, and he begged him to guide his steps in the way of Truth. Mullá 'Alí tried to calm him and persuaded him to return to his shop, and he did so.

The father of this inspired young man became very angry with his son when he heard about what had happened, and he did all he could to persuade him to give up what he believed to be strange ideas. His father went so far as to chase down Mullá 'Alí, and beat him severely for influencing his son, an act which he later came to deeply regret. All of this was a great test for the young shopkeeper, but he remained a spiritually transformed man. Eventually, he became a devoted follower of Bahá'u'lláh, and some time later he was brutally martyred for his Faith. His name is 'Abdu'l-Vahháb, the one who received his Charter of Liberty, and one so worthy to be enrolled among the stalwart band of the Heroes of the new Age.

This was only the beginning of Mullá 'Alí's suffering in the path of the Báb. He was beaten, chained, imprisoned, and finally forced to leave the land. The last report of him tells of his banishment as a prisoner and exile to Turkey, where he was put on trial and sentenced to hard labour on the docks of Istanbul. The manner of his death is not known, nevertheless Mullá 'Alí earned the everlasting honour of having been the first to suffer and to lay down his life for the new-born Faith of God.

Next, the Báb sent fourteen Letters of the Living

throughout the country to announce the good news of the new Day of God. He instructed each one to send back to Him the names of all the people who believed in Him; these names He would record. Then He called Mullá Ḥusayn, the first Letter of the Living, to come to Him.

Mullá Ḥusayn knelt before the Báb and listened while He explained his special mission. First, he was to raise the cry, 'Awake, awake, for, lo! the Gate is open, and the morning Light is shedding its radiance upon all mankind!' To those who responded to his call he would teach the new Cause of God. The second part of his mission was even more important. The Báb told him to travel to Tehran, the capital of Persia, and search for a Holy Mystery there. That mystery was none other than the One for Whom the Báb was preparing the way; Mullá Ḥusayn was to have the honour of ensuring that the announcement of the Báb be delivered to Him. Mullá Ḥusayn obeyed every word spoken to him by the Báb, for he understood that the voice of the Báb was the same as the voice of God.

After travelling from city to city teaching of the new Day of God, he finally arrived in Tehran. There, he asked everyone he met where he might find one who was known to be holy, pure, wise and kind-hearted. In time he met a man who said he knew of such a person who went by the name of Ḥusayn 'Alí. He said that He was known for His good deeds and pure life. The people called Him the 'Father of the Poor'. When Mullá Ḥusayn heard this, he knew he had found the 'Mystery' he had been searching for. He asked the man if he would carry a scroll of the writings of the Báb to Ḥusayn 'Alí; the man answered that he would certainly do so. The 'Mystery', Ḥusayn 'Alí, was none other than Bahá'u'lláh, for Ḥusayn 'Alí would take the name Bahá'u'lláh in the future.

The man went to the house of Bahá'u'lláh, and was welcomed in, having announced the purpose of his visit. He was then taken into the presence of Bahá'u'lláh. The brother of Bahá'u'lláh was standing nearby, so the man presented the scroll to him, and he laid it before Bahá'u'lláh. Bahá'u'lláh picked it up and began to read. After reading but a few lines of this writing of the Báb, Bahá'u'lláh, without the least hesitation, accepted and declared that the Báb was the prophet of God, and that anyone who failed to recognize the Divine origin of these words had strayed far from the path of justice. One need only read these words written by Bahá'u'lláh about the Báb to understand that He was ready to give His all for Him: 'I stand, life in hand, ready; that perchance, through God's loving-kindness and grace, this revealed and manifest Letter may lay down His life as a sacrifice in the path of the Primal Point, the Most Exalted Word.'

Before the man left, Bahá'u'lláh gave him a small gift and asked that he return and give it to Mullá Ḥusayn as a token of His appreciation and love. The man returned and presented the gift to Mullá Ḥusayn. Filled with emotion as he took the gift from the man, Mullá Ḥusayn held it gently in his hand, and softly kissed it. He then kissed the eyes of the man who had done him so great a favour in fulfilling this task, eyes that had looked upon Bahá'u'lláh, and he prayed that God would grant him eternal happiness for having done him so great a favour.

Mullá Ḥusayn soon sent a message to the Báb that Bahá'u'lláh was now a defender of His Cause. This news was the source of supreme happiness for the Báb, because it meant that His Cause was complete in every way, and that nothing could succeed in preventing it from achieving its purpose. After the Báb would sacrifice His own life for His Cause, Bahá'u'lláh would guard and bring it to completion. Bahá'u'lláh, the Glory of God, was the very one for Whom the Báb was the Gate, for Whom He was preparing the way, and through Whom God would deliver all mankind from error. Bahá'u'lláh would fulfil the Báb's covenant with His followers.

Now only Quddús remained with the Báb. The Báb chose him to be His companion on His journey to the holy city of Mecca, in Arabia, far away from His native land of Persia. The Báb saved this most difficult teaching mission for Himself. In this holy city He hoped to light anew the fire of God, a fire that had all but completely died out. He and Quddús would go together.

After a difficult journey over land and sea, the Báb and Quddús reached at last the holy city of Mecca. In the centre of this city stands a large black cube-shaped stone building. Legend says that the remains of the Prophet Abraham are buried at this spot, and the Prophet Muḥammad revealed that it was the point toward which prayers were to be offered. Therefore, many people came as pilgrims from distant lands to walk solemnly around this building. Once a person completed this pilgrimage, he would add the title 'Haj' before his name to show he had done so. The man chosen to take care of the holy city and be in charge of the visiting pilgrims was called the Sherif of Mecca.

The Báb had joined the thousands of other pilgrims circling around the huge, black structure when suddenly He stopped at its door. Seizing the ring hanging on it, He called out in a clear voice three times that He was the promised Prophet Whose coming they had been waiting for. A hush of shock fell upon the circling multitudes when they heard this announcement. Later, when these pilgrims returned to the various lands from which they had come, some of them spread this news among their countrymen.

The final act of the Báb while at Mecca was to ensure that the Sherif of the city be informed of this great announcement. He addressed a letter to the Sherif in which He explained the purpose of His mission and called upon him to join His Cause. He handed this letter and some of His other Writings over to Quddús, instructing him to deliver them to the Sherif. This Quddús faithfully did, but, unfortunately, the Sherif was too busy with the things of this world to give proper attention to the things of God, so he failed to respond as he should have. It was not until several years later, after the martyrdom of the Báb, that he did read these Holy Writings and understood their purpose. Upon learning of the suffering and martyrdom of the Báb, he asked for the curse of God to come upon His persecutors, persecutors whom he described as an 'evil people . . . who, in days past, treated in the same manner our holy and illustrious ancestors'.

One more important thing happened on the road from

Mecca. The Báb was riding a donkey, and Quddús was walking before Him. It was here that the Báb had a vision. In this vision the souls of all the holy men who had died in glory for God in the olden days appeared to Him. They warned Him not to return to His homeland, for danger awaited Him there. To them the Báb replied, 'I am come into this world to bear witness to the glory of sacrifice . . . Rejoice, for both I and Quddús will be slain on the altar of our devotion to the King of Glory . . . The drops of this consecrated blood will be the seed out of which will arise the mighty Tree of God, the Tree that will gather beneath its all embracing shadow the peoples and kindreds of the earth.'

It was nine months before the Báb and Quddús returned to their homeland, landing at the coastal city of Bushehr. After a short rest, the Báb spoke with the faithful Quddús. The Báb told him that the days of their companionship on earth had come to an end, but that they would be together forever in that heavenly kingdom, beyond this life on earth, of never-failing joy and brightness. He asked him to raise his spirit in happiness, for God had chosen him to suffer most for God's sake and be at the very front of that divine army, soon to arise, that would choose death to this world rather than abandon the Cause of God. The Báb foretold how he, Quddús, would remain in this world long enough to be in the presence of the very One He, the Báb, was announcing to the peoples of the world, none other than Bahá'u'lláh, the Glory of God. He assured him that when he attained to that Presence, all harm and pain would pass away and be forgotten, for to attain the presence of Bahá'u'lláh was to attain the presence of the Manifestation of God on earth. With these thrilling last words, the Báb sent forth Quddús, the young hero of God, to the inland city of Shiraz, where he was to teach the Cause of God.

We may well imagine how the heart of Quddús must have sung as he set out upon his journey. What boldness must have marked his step, what certitude must have set upon his brow, what power must have filled his very being! No sooner had he arrived at Shiraz than he met with an uncle of the Báb. This uncle had not yet accepted his nephew as the awaited Prophet of God. Quddús spoke to him with convincing truth, explaining the teachings of his kinsman, the Báb. Listening with an open heart to the noble Quddús, this uncle came to believe in the Báb and was enrolled as the first believer of that city. So strong became his faith that he set his whole life on serving the Báb. He was a successful merchant; nevertheless, he let nothing come between him and service to his new-found Faith. Later, this was amply proven when he gave his life rather than say he did not believe in the Báb. This story is told in Chapter 6, 'The Seven Heroes of God at Tehran'. This uncle's name is Ḥájí Mírzá Siyyid 'Alí.

The next person Quddús met was an old man named Mullá Ṣádiq. He was the priest of a mosque with a large membership. Quddús was carrying some writings of the Báb, which he showed to him. Mullá Ṣádiq instantly recognized that these writings could be nothing but the Word of God.

Having believed on the spot, he became so filled with

the spirit of faith that he decided to put the words of the Báb into immediate effect. One of his duties as priest was to lead his congregation in daily prayer in the mosque. He decided that he would change the prayer and recite it as the Báb said it should be done. The worshippers had gathered before him, ready to be led in prayer. As he chanted the prayer he added additional words of the Báb. When the people of the congregation heard these words they broke into commotion and raised an uproar against what he had done. This prayer had been said the same way for more than a thousand years, and they could not imagine that it could ever be changed.

Quickly, the news of what had happened spread across the city. When the authorities heard of it, they became so upset that they ordered the arrest of Mullá Ṣádiq along with one of his ex-students, Mullá 'Alí-Akbar, and Quddús. These three were brought before the authorities for questioning. It was decided that they deserved to be punished horribly before all the townspeople. First they stripped old Mullá Ṣádiq and then whipped him with one thousand lashes. Next they ordered that the beards of all three be burnt off. Finally, they had holes cut through their noses, leashes run through the bleeding holes, and then they were led, leash in hand, through the streets of the city. The awful spectacle over, they were run out of town with the warning that if they ever returned they would be crucified on the spot.

One might wonder why such awful punishments were ordered by the authorities for such a seemingly small thing as changing a prayer. It is because many people, often those in authority, never want to see religious customs change, so they resist such change by every means within their power. This attitude is one of the chief reasons the life of the Prophet of God is filled with woe. God gives Him the power to do whatever He wishes, but most of the leaders of the old religions do not want to understand, therefore they oppose Him. The other reason is that they want to maintain their stranglehold over the thoughts and consciences of the people. Also, the cruelty of the authorities towards the people in those backward times made things awful for everybody.

The news of these events spread like wildfire throughout the kingdom. The people wanted to know exactly who was this young man, the Bab. Soon word of the religion of the Báb reached the ear of the Shah. Hoping to get to the truth of the matter, the Shah decided to send an investigator to meet and interview the Báb. He chose his wisest and most trusted counsellor to undertake this mission. This man's name was Vaḥíd. His orders were to go and meet the Báb, investigate His claim and report his findings back to the Shah. Vaḥíd, like many others, including the Báb, had the right to use the title 'Siyyid', which meant that he was descended from the family of the Prophet Muhammad. Vaḥíd met and spoke with the Báb three times. He planned to convince the Báb to give up his claim of prophethood and take him back to Tehran as proof of the success of his mission.

'When I came into His presence,' recounted Vaḥíd later, 'and heard His words, the opposite of that which I had imagined took place. In the course of my first audience

23

with Him, I was utterly abashed and confounded; by the end of the second, I felt as helpless and ignorant as a child; the third found me as lowly as the dust beneath His feet. He had indeed ceased to be the contemptible siyyid I had previously imagined. To me, He was the Manifestation of God Himself, the living embodiment of the Divine Spirit. Ever since that day, I have yearned to lay down my life for His sake. I rejoice that the day I have longed to witness is fast approaching.'

He did not even bother to return to report to the Shah. When no word was heard of him, the governor of the province went looking for Vaḥíd. When he found him he asked if he had fallen under the spell of the Báb. Vaḥíd answered that no one but God could capture his heart, and that His Word was unquestionably the Word of Truth. Vaḥíd meant what he said, for in the end, the day he longed to witness came to pass, and he too gave his life for his Faith. This story will be told in Chapter 7, 'Vaḥíd: Hero of God at Nayríz'.

Yet another to join the fast-spreading Faith of the Báb was a man known as Ḥujjat, of Zanján. He had become famous for his knowledge of the sacred books, his absolute honesty, and for speaking out courageously for what he believed to be the truth. His fame and knowledge attracted to him a large number of students and followers. As soon as he heard of the Báb and that He claimed to be a new Messenger from God, Ḥujjat decided to look into the matter. He selected one of his trusted students to travel to Shiraz, meet with the Báb, investigate the truth of His claim and return and report to him. Attaining the

24

presence of the Báb, the student stayed for forty days learning the principles of the Faith and feeling the power of the Báb, but he did not become a Bábí, as the followers of the Báb were called.

The student returned at the very moment when Ḥujjat was meeting with the leading priests of the city. As soon as he appeared Ḥujjat asked him whether he believed in the Báb, or not. His student replied that he would follow whatever Ḥujjat decided on the matter. This reply angered Ḥujjat. He told him that had they not been in the presence of so many guests he would have punished him for making such a statement. 'How dare you', asked Ḥujjat, 'consider matters of belief to be dependent upon the approbation or rejection of others?'

During this conversation the student had been holding a sacred writing of the Báb. Ḥujjat took it from his hand and began to read. He had barely finished one page of that holy Tablet when he bowed down to the ground right in front of everyone and, in a loud, clear voice, swore his allegiance to the Báb. He said that whomever denied Him he would regard as having denied God Himself.

Imagine how amazed everyone present must have been when their leader and teacher did such a thing and made such a statement. This proves that souls who are ready to know the truth of God are attracted through one word. Ḥujjat was deadly serious about this pledge, for he was destined, after great agony, to surrender his life for the cause of the Báb. This story is told in Chapter 8, 'Ḥujjat: Captain of the Heroes of God at Zanján'.

CHAPTER FOUR

THE BÁB IS IMPRISONED AND A HEROINE OF GOD ANNOUNCES THE NEW DAY

More and more people from all walks of life were becoming Bábís, including such famous people as Bahá'u'lláh, Vaḥíd, and Ḥujjat. The government authorities began to get worried. They were afraid that if the Báb became too popular it would upset the way things had been done for hundreds of years. They thought that if He was locked up in some far-off place then the whole thing would die out. They chose a prison in the farthest corner of the kingdom, at a place called Máh-Kú. But this did not work, because even in this forgotten place the spiritual power of the personality of the Báb began to have its effect. Each day the villagers would come to receive His blessing, and His guard came to love Him dearly. Soon, more and more of His followers began arriving from distant parts of the land to simply gaze upon their Beloved. Mullá Ḥusayn, who in his travels had been inviting receptive souls to the new religion of God, walked more than a thousand miles to be with Him again.

Spies for the government had been watching all of

this; they reported that the Prisoner was just as popular as ever and that people were treating Him as if He was their Lord. Further alarmed, the authorities decided to march Him off to a different prison and guard Him more closely than before. The place was in the north of Persia, at the isolated castle of Chihríq. But, it was too late. The fame of the Báb was spreading so fast that nothing could stop it. As before, people began arriving from every corner of the land; as before, villagers on their way to their daily work would gather at the castle walls calling on the name and blessing of the Báb. Good priests, officials and plain folks of the area, their hearts captured by the young Prophet of God, began embracing His religion. One man, following the instructions given him in a vision by the Báb, came on foot all the way from India to find his Beloved.

Among those who heard of the Báb was an official by the name of Dayyán. He had defeated in argument anyone who tried to convince him of the truth of the Báb. Then one night he had a dream in which he dreamt of two sacred verses. Telling no one of it, he decided to send a letter to the Báb to see if He could know what he had dreamt of. To make it as difficult as possible, the letter made no mention of the dream, but merely said that he had some things in mind, and he would be interested to know if the Báb could tell him what they were. Dayyán soon received his answer from the pen of the all-knowing Báb Himself. Reading the mind of Dayyán, the Báb explained to him everything he had dreamt of and even quoted perfectly to him the two sacred verses in the dream. Upon reading this answer, Dayyán accepted the

Faith of the Báb and decided to walk on foot, as a sign of his respect, all the way to the castle of <u>Ch</u>ihríq to see Him. His meeting with the Báb confirmed his faith, and he showed a fiery love for every moment thereafter. Eventually he suffered martyrdom at the orders of one of the worst enemies of the Faith of God.

When imprisonment failed to silence the Báb or prevent the spread of His new-born religion, the chief minister of the Shah, the Grand Vizier, became very angry. Everything he had tried to do to stop the Báb had failed. Then he thought of a new plan – make the Báb look ridiculous by putting Him on trial before important religious judges.

The trial was to be held in the town of Tabriz, a few days' journey from the prison where the Báb was being held. While on the road, He and His guards stopped at a small village for the night. The fame of the Báb had gone before Him, so all the townspeople were waiting to see Him when He arrived.

A prince who happened to be staying in the village decided to test the power and courage of the Báb. His idea was to give Him a wild horse to ride and watch what would happen. He knew this horse was dangerous, because it had thrown the most skilful horsemen, but he gave the Báb no warning. All eyes were on the Báb as He mounted the horse, looking to see what would happen. At His gentle touch and sweet voice, that fierce beast became as docile as a tame pony; He rode it to and fro as He wished! Imagine how amazed everyone was! Strange is it not that a simple beast knows the voice of its master, while the worldly-wise are heedless of the voice of their Lord?

Reaching the town of Tabriz, the Báb was brought before the judges. Their plan was to make Him look as foolish as possible. Striding majestically into the courtroom, the Báb took the seat reserved for the prince. As He gazed around at those gathered for the trial, power and authority blazed from His eyes. For a moment not one person dared to say a word. Finally, one of the priests mustered enough courage to speak.

'Who', he asked, 'do you claim to be and what is the message which you have brought?'

The voice of God thundering from His mouth, the Báb answered, 'I am, I am, I am the promised One! I am the One whose name you have for a thousand years invoked . . . and the hour of whose Revelation you have prayed God to hasten. Verily I say, it is incumbent upon the peoples of both the East and the West to obey My word . . .' The plan to humiliate the Báb had failed. Instead of shaming the Báb, the trial only served to dramatically and publicly proclaim, for the first time, His stupendous announcement to mankind.

The plan to discredit the Báb having failed, the priests were completely beside themselves as to what to do next. One of them, crazed with rage and filled with envy, expressed his deepest fear about the Báb. He said that unless they acted quickly, everyone would believe in the Báb and then He would take over the whole area. Not really knowing what to do, they decided to punish Him with the dreaded 'bastinado'. The guards were ordered to lay the Báb on His back, raise His legs, and beat His bare feet with a stick. At the last moment the guard assigned to do the beating refused to commit such an outrage. He believed the Báb to be innocent of any wrongdoing. Wild with anger, the head priest took the rod in his own hand and began whipping the feet. So enraged was he that one of the blows struck the blessed face of the Báb! O! how foolish are those who oppose the Messenger of God. They seek to injure the very One who has come to lead them to lasting happiness! This shameful treatment of the young Prophet of God over, they returned Him to the castle-prison of Chihríq.

In all, the Báb was imprisoned for more than three years. During this time He was able to write the main book of His religion, the Bayán. This book contained the new laws the followers of the Báb were to follow; but more importantly it indicated that Bahá'u'lláh would fulfil His Cause after His martyrdom. The Báb referred to Bahá'u'lláh as 'Him whom God would make manifest'. In this book the Báb made it clear that all of his followers must recognize and accept Bahá'u'lláh as soon as He made Himself known to them. Bahá'u'lláh would complete the divine mission of establishing peace and order throughout the world under the almighty Law of God. This was the Covenant of the Báb with His followers.

Another important event happened while the Báb was in prison. A group of His disciples gathered at a small town called Badasht. They were to meet for twenty-two days. Quddús and Ṭáhirih were present, but it was Bahá'u'lláh Who was to lead the conference. One of the main purposes of the conference was to show that the Faith of the Báb and the new laws revealed in His book the Bayán were not merely a spiritual revival, but rather, the beginning of the new religion of God on earth! This meant to close the door of the past and open it to the future; it meant to ring in the new Day of God and ring out the old; it meant the end of priests running religion in secret; it meant the end of false religious ideas; it meant the end of using religion in a destructive way. And who was to sound this call? None other than that stainless woman and Letter of the Living, Ṭáhirih. Here is how she did it.

One of the customs of the old religion followed in that part of the world was that women and girls were to wear a veil to cover their face when men were present. Also, they had to sit out of sight when the men were meeting. To do otherwise was considered to go against God. Some people find it hard to understand such a custom, but for the people of that day it was a strict, unbreakable practice passed down from their forefathers from time immemorial. The new laws of God brought by the Báb taught that none of this was necessary any longer. Ṭáhirih was ready, completely ready, to obey the laws of the new era.

Bahá'u'lláh knew that many of those attending the conference did not fully understand the revolutionary character of the religion of the Báb, and that they were not ready to break with all of the religious traditions of the past. A plan was conceived to lessen the alarm and confusion such a realization would arouse. Ṭáhirih and Quddús agreed that she would proclaim the independent character of the Revelation of the Báb and emphasize the changes in the laws of the old religion. Quddús, on the other hand, was to oppose her and reject her views. Bahá'u'lláh, although the prime mover of all of the events which took place at the memorable conference, would take a neutral attitude in the controversy.

Near the end of the conference the scene was set to put the plan into effect. Bahá'u'lláh lay ill upon His bed and Quddús and the other men were gathered about Him. A messenger entered and handed Quddús an invitation from Ṭáhirih inviting him to visit her in a garden nearby. Refusing the invitation, he got into a disagreement with the messenger. Suddenly, Ṭáhirih, unveiled and breathtakingly beautiful, swept gracefully into their midst and sat down next to Quddús. The men were doubly shocked – first because she had the audacity to enter a gathering of the men, and, second, because she was without a veil. As they sat staring in disbelief, she proclaimed in ringing, trumpet-like tones that this was the beginning of the new Day of God. Quddús jumped to his feet, sword in hand, acting as if he might strike her down on the spot.

The effect she made on the men was instant and decisive. Those not ready to accept the drastic changes brought by the Báb were torn and distressed by such a thought. One went so far as to slit his own throat and, with blood streaming down the front of his clothes, rush away from her presence. Others, unable to bear the thought of such far-reaching changes, denied their new-found faith and fled from the conference. Her purpose completed, she thereupon invited the remaining companions to embrace and celebrate the dawn of the New Day.

The tension continued for a few days until Bahá'u'lláh stepped in and healed the wounds of this controversy, directing everyone's footsteps along the path of constructive service to the Cause of God.

So it happened that the unprepared were separated from the prepared, the obedient from the disobedient, the wholehearted from the half-hearted, the sheep from the goats. Fulfilling its purpose, the conference ended, and those remaining went their separate ways to teach the Cause of the Báb.

Some time later, Ṭáhirih was swept into the storm of terror that was soon to engulf the religion of the Báb. She was held under arrest in the house of an important official while government officials questioned her about her new beliefs. With burning passion and without the least hesitation she proclaimed her faith in the Revelation of the Báb. Nevertheless, because of his fear that the Bábís might destroy the government, the Grand Vizier ordered that she be put to death. She was taken outside, strangled with her own scarf and thrown into a well. But before they committed the evil deed she turned to her tormentors and boldly declared, 'You can kill me as soon as you like, but you cannot stop the emancipation of women.' And thus she died a martyr's death.

Her tormentors hoped that would be the end of her, but it was not. Her clarion call has risen from her martyrdom, has steadily gained in power, and now reverberates from land to land announcing to all the peoples the New Day of God and the equality of women with men.

In this chapter we have seen how, during His

imprisonment, the Báb was able to proclaim His mission publicly, reveal His Holy Book, the Bayán, and make His covenant concerning Bahá'u'lláh; how the spread of His fame could not be stopped, and how the independent character of the new Faith of God was made plain at the Conference of Badasht. Now the story of the things that happened during the last months of the Báb's stay in prison will be told.

CHAPTER FIVE

THE HEROES OF GOD AT FORT ṬABARSÍ

It so happened that during his teaching journey Quddús was detained and forced to remain for several months in the house of one of the enemies of God. When the Báb heard of this He sent a message to Mullá Ḥusayn telling him to go and rescue Quddús. Obeying the Báb, Mullá Ḥusayn mounted his horse and with two hundred and two companions began the march to release Quddús. The road they travelled passed through several villages. All along the way Mullá Ḥusayn and his fellow Bábís would call the villagers to the new Day of God. Many responded, and became Bábís. A number of men decided to join the march to free Quddús. All went well until they came to the town of Barfurush.

The religious leader of this town especially feared and hated Quddús and the followers of the Báb because of an earlier event. Quddús, who had been born and raised in this town, had returned to inform the head priest of the coming of 'The Lord of the Age' and invite him to embrace the Cause of the Báb. The priest refused the invitation himself, but then, to his dismay, he witnessed, through the efforts of Quddús, the conversion of more than three hundred of the townspeople to the Cause of God within a week! These events made him fear that his power over the people and the source of his wealth would end.

The head priest's fears were renewed when he heard that the Bábís were approaching to pass through his town. He decided to take action to prevent them from winning any more of the townspeople over to the Cause of the Báb. Calling to his mosque as many of the people as would come, he ranted and raved against the Bábís until he had excited the people into a frenzy of fear. He shouted that the Bábís would soon be at their doors to take everything they owned, and that no one would be left alive unless they destroyed them. The people, not ever expecting that their priest would lie to them, did what he told them to do.

So it was that an angry mob, armed to the teeth, greeted Mullá Ḥusayn and his companions as they approached the town. Brandishing their weapons, these misguided folks cursed and insulted the arriving Bábís. Fearing they might be attacked at any moment, the companions of Mullá Ḥusayn took measures to defend themselves. Mullá Ḥusayn told them to hold their swords unless they were forced to use them. No sooner had he said this than the mob opened fire, sending a barrage of musket balls slamming into the companions; six fell wounded to the ground. The gallant men of Mullá Ḥusayn begged him to permit them to defend themselves, but again he commanded them to hold, for he desired to avoid shedding the blood of these poor, misguided people.

At that moment a bullet struck a dear friend standing

at the side of Mullá Ḥusayn, and he fell dead at his feet. This man had walked for miles at his side and had shared all of his hardships and successes. The murder of his friend brought Mullá Ḥusayn's patience to an end. Raising his eyes to heaven, he called to God, 'Behold, O God, my God, the plight of Thy chosen companions, and witness the welcome these people have accorded Thy loved one.' With that, he drew his sword, spurred his horse, and charged all alone into the centre of the enemy forces.

His first target was the one who had just shot and killed the friend standing at his side. Seeing Mullá Ḥusayn charging with raised sword in his direction, the man tried to take cover behind a tree. Galloping at full speed, the man sharply in his sights, Mullá Ḥusayn let his sword begin its mighty stroke. The man raised his gun to stop the blow, but its tremendous sweep cut tree, man and gun completely through. Seeing the bravery and power of Mullá Ḥusayn, the remaining enemy retreated in panic and fear.

The courage of God blazing from his eyes, galloping through their midst, bullets raining from the air, Mullá Ḥusayn rode into the city, cutting down any who blocked his way. He headed for the house of the priest who had caused all of this trouble. Reaching the house without a scratch, he galloped three times around it challenging the priest to come out and face him. The cowardly priest hid in the house quaking with fear; it would be suicide to face Mullá Ḥusayn man to man in battle.

Now all the townspeople called for Peace! Peace! At the same time the companions of Mullá Ḥusayn caught up to him. They had given up hope of ever finding him alive after watching him charge off alone into the whole mob. How surprised they were to see him safe and sound and master of the town! 'O Lord of the Age!' they cried, referring to the Promised One, the Báb, 'O Lord of the Age!' Mullá Ḥusayn granted the town peace, but not until he had castigated them for receiving him and his companions with bullets instead of proper hospitality.

He and his companions decided to stay at a nearby inn to rest before continuing on their mission to rescue Quddús. Little did they suspect that as soon as they went to the inn, the same trouble-making priest crept out of his house and again began to stir up some of the people against them.

That evening Mullá Ḥusayn tried three times to send one of his men to the roof of the inn to chant the evening prayer. Each was killed in his turn by a sniper's bullet! The enemy had broken their word and surrounded the inn. Renewing their attack, they had double-crossed the Bábís. Having lost his patience with these faithless people, Mullá Ḥusayn leaped upon his horse and shouted to his companions, 'Mount your steeds, O heroes of God!' Forward he led the charge, slashing the enemy on the right and on the left. They were punished dearly for breaking their word. Those who escaped with their lives scattered in panic before the swords of the lion-hearted Mullá Ḥusayn and his men. As the sun went down, the field of battle was commanded by the Heroes of God. What a fearsome sight it was to see the dead lying here and there as proof of their victory.

After this awful lesson, some of the more sensible citizens of the town came to Mullá Ḥusayn begging for peace. They asked that all be forgiven, and that he and his men go on their way undisturbed. One among them, a man named K̲h̲usraw, pretended to be friendly and offered to guide the Bábís on their journey through an unknown forest. He was accompanied by his own crew of armed horsemen. Actually, K̲h̲usraw had been sent by the crazed priest to kill them at the first opportunity. Mullá Ḥusayn agreed to the offer, but he warned the treacherous K̲h̲usraw that 'if ye do evil, the evil will return upon you'.

After travelling a distance into the forest, the Bábís became scattered along the forest trails. Heedless of the warning of Mullá Ḥusayn, K̲h̲usraw had planned that the Bábís be separated and hunted down singly by his men. The sound of musket-fire revealed the treachery of K̲h̲usraw, and several Bábís were killed before they could regroup to defend themselves. Hearing the musket-fire, Mullá Ḥusayn dismounted and ordered that the call to prayer be sounded to gather his scattered men together. The treacherous K̲h̲usraw was killed on the spot by one of Mullá Ḥusayn's men. Burning with anger because of his treachery, the Bábís now turned their wrath upon the horsemen; raising the battle cry 'O Lord of the Age!', in one onslaught they struck down all K̲h̲usraw's crew, except one who was left alive. This one was spared because he was a defenceless servant. Mullá Ḥusayn sent him back to the town of Barfurush to tell the people how what had happened was as a result of K̲h̲usraw's treachery.

The next morning at daybreak, after Mullá Ḥusayn had offered his prayers, he gathered his companions together and said something to them that indicated what was to soon happen to them. 'We are approaching our Karbila, our ultimate destination,' he said. Karbila was a place where a famous spiritual battle had taken place long ago. When the Heroes heard this they knew that a glorious end awaited them. It meant that they were to repeat this most famous of heroic battles from the olden days, and were to make the same spiritual sacrifice as was made then.

(Dear reader, we shall now make a break in our story and turn back the clock to those olden days over a thousand years earlier to learn of the battle and sacrifice of the Heroes of God of that day, of the Imam Husayn and his companions. This will help us to better understand the mighty deeds of the Heroes of God told about in this book.)

****

This is how it happened. More than 1,300 years ago the religion of the Prophet Muhammad, Islam, had fallen under control of the enemies of God of that day. The grandson of the Prophet was named Husayn. Like his father before him, he had the title of Imam, which meant he was the chosen spiritual leader of the followers of Islam.

A pure-hearted young man, Husayn's only desire was that the people be allowed to live the kind of religious life his Grandfather had said God wanted for them. The enemies of God had taken control of Islam and for a long time they tried to get Husayn to promise he would obey them; but he would have nothing to do with them. Many people had grown tired of their cruelty and hoped Husayn would do something to restore the true Faith of his Grandfather. They sent letters and messengers to Husayn begging him to come to the city of Kufah and take his rightful place as the chosen leader of Islam. He decided to accept their invitation.

Ignoring warnings of danger, he did what he had to do. He packed up his family, children included, gathered some of his followers, and began a journey by horse and camel across a great semi-desert in Iraq. He set out for the city of Kufah where an evil governor ruled. His party consisted of fewer than one hundred souls, of whom about 72 were armed men. His mission was to preserve the spirit of the true Faith of his Grandfather; this he would do through his own martyrdom, for he had been chosen by God to be sacrificed to ensure that good would overcome evil and redeem the peoples of the earth for their sins and injustices. His martyrdom was destined to occur at a place known as Karbila in the land of Iraq on the road to Kufah.

When the news of the coming of the Imam Husayn reached the wicked governor, he decided to take action to prevent Husayn from completing his mission. Fearing loss of his position and power, he let it be known that anyone who supported Husayn would be tortured and put to death. He ordered that a troop of 1,000 horsemen be sent to intercept Husayn's party and bring them under guard to him. The captain of the horsemen was named Hurr. When Hurr arrived he was treated with kindness by Husayn, and Husayn led Hurr and his men in prayer. After a discussion between them, Husayn's party was allowed to continue to the place known as Karbila. Hurr and his men followed behind. There, at Karbila, Husayn pitched his tents for the last time.

Next day an army of several thousand, consisting of archers, soldiers, cavalry and spearmen, arrived on the scene. Their orders were to force Husayn to pledge his allegiance to the leader of the enemies of God. This, of course, he could never do. The army surrounded Husayn's party, cutting them off from the only supply of water. For several days Husayn tried to convince them to let them pass in peace, but the enemy would not relent. Instead, they prepared for battle. His family and companions began to suffer from thirst.

Husayn approached the forces gathered before him and addressed them. He began by praising God, then he reminded them of the words of his Grandfather, Prophet Muhammad, concerning himself and his brother: 'These are the two lords of the youths of the inhabitants of heaven.' He named those present who had heard these words with their own ears from the mouth of the Prophet, Muhammad. So powerful was the truth of what he said that many of the opposing forces were moved in sympathy for him. Hurr, captain of the troop which had first intercepted him, realized the truth of what he said. Suddenly he shouted, 'I have been given the choice between

Heaven and Hell. By God, I will not choose anything before Heaven even though I be cut to pieces and burnt.' With that, he spurred on his horse and galloped over to the side of Husayn. He died a glorious death defending the true Faith of God that day. And because of the choice he made his name will never be forgotten, and his story will always stir the breast of every soul who thirsts after righteousness.

Then the fighting began. Hurr was one of the first of the supporters of Husayn to step forward in defence of the surrounded party in mortal, man-to-man combat. Quickly a furious battle ensued. Arrows began flying in every direction, swords flashed in the sunlight, and the horsemen came charging, thrusting their spears at the Heroes of God. Hopelessly outnumbered, one by one, fighting to their last breath, the supporters of Husayn fell. Finally, only Husayn, his family and half-brother remained alive. While attempting to get water for the thirsty women and children, his half-brother was killed. Now only Husayn and the women and children remained. Carrying his infant son in his arms he pleaded for water for the child. At that moment an arrow pierced the baby's throat, killing him.

Then the bloodthirsty enemy closed in on Husayn, hacking at him with swords and shooting arrows into him. Valiantly he resisted the fierce onslaught, but at last, with blood pouring from his numerous wounds, he fell face down on the dust, and the final dreadful blow was delivered, severing his head from his body. Pitilessly, the horsemen trampled his precious remains under their horses' hooves.

In the midst of his agony he spoke these words: 'Thou knowest, O my Beloved, that I have abandoned the world for Thy sake, and have ,placed my trust in Thee alone. I am impatient to hasten to Thee, for the beauty of Thy countenance has been unveiled to my eyes. Thou dost witness the evil designs which my wicked persecutor has cherished against me. Nay, never will I submit to his wishes or pledge my allegiance to him.'

(These words would be repeated by his descendant Siyyid Vaḥíd centuries later. This story is told in Chapter 7, 'Vaḥíd: Hero of God at Nayríz'.)

The women and children were taken prisoner, and the heads of Husayn and his brave companions were cut off and raised on the ends of spears and taken to Kufah to be shown to the wicked governor. Looking at the head of Husayn, the governor raised a stick he held in his hand and struck it upon the sacred mouth of the head, remarking that the look of that mouth reminded him of the mouth of the Prophet Muhammad, which he had seen years before. Oh! what evil lurks in the hearts of the the enemies of God! Thus ended a spiritual drama that would not be repeated until the cleansing force of God was set loose again through the Báb.

****

Now let us return to the Heroes of God of our own day, and the story of Mullá Ḥusayn. After hearing the story just told, we can imagine the strong effect of Mullá Ḥusayn's statement to his men that they were approaching their own 'Karbila'. The memory of a story so familiar to them of that first Husayn, and what happened to him at Karbila so long ago, must have welled up in their minds. These thoughts, no doubt, livened their spirits. They were urged by Mullá Ḥusayn 'to arrive at that hallowed spot in a state of complete detachment, wholly sanctified from all that pertains to this world'. The place destined to be their Karbila was the Shrine of S͟hayk͟h Ṭabarsí where the remains of a saintly man by this name were entombed. It was located in a forested area with hills, villages and mountains all around.

When they arrived, the keeper of the shrine threw himself devotedly at the feet of Mullá Ḥusayn. Mullá Ḥusayn seated him at his side and the keeper told him of a dream he had the night before. He told how in the dream the Imam Husayn of old had arrived at the shrine with his warriors. There they remained and fought the most heroic battles, just as they had done in the times of old. And that the Prophet of God, Himself, arrived one night and joined that blessed company. He said that the face of Mullá Ḥusayn was the very face of the Imam Husayn he had seen in his dream. After listening to the story of the dream told by the keeper of the shrine, Mullá Ḥusayn assured him that each of the glorious scenes he had witnessed in his dream would come to pass before his very eyes.

Towards evening on the first night of their arrival, a savage crowd appeared out of the woods. They threatened to put every one of them to the sword to avenge the death of K͟husraw. Some of the Bábís drew their swords and leaped to take up the challenge. Putting the enemy to flight, they pursued them into the darkness. Thinking they had followed the enemy to their haven, they entered a village, and a commotion ensued. In the confusion that followed, some innocent people and the mother of the owner of the village were killed. Then the Bábís learned of their tragic mistake: they were in the wrong village! Their enemy was not there at all! They had shed the blood of innocent people!

The leader of the Bábí troop was horrified at the grievous mistake. He begged forgiveness for the dreadful error they had made, and he tried to explain to the owner of the village, who was called Naẓar, how the tragedy had come about. Naẓar, who had suffered the loss of his mother, was convinced of the Bábís' honest intentions and was deeply impressed by the spiritual fire that motivated them. He asked to be taken to meet Mullá Ḥusayn.

At the hour of dawn they arrived at the Shrine of Shaykh Ṭabarsí. After hearing of the tragic mistake, Mullá Ḥusayn expressed to Naẓar in the most touching language the sympathy which he and his companions felt for his loss. He then proceeded to recount to him the entire story of the mission they had undertaken and how this defensive measure had led to this awful mistake. Again he assured him of the sorrow which the death of Naẓar's mother had caused him. So moved was Naẓar by the story of their mission and the sincerity of Mullá Ḥusayn that he spontaneously pledged his undying loyalty to the Cause of the Lord of the Age. He returned to his village and prepared whatever provisions the companions might require.

One cannot but be amazed how, through the sheer force of sincerity and truth, a man who had every reason to despise the Bábís was won over to their side and became a valued supporter!

The unfortunate event made right, Mullá Ḥusayn wasted no time getting busy. To protect his companions in the coming battles, he ordered that plans be made to construct a fort around the shrine, and he put his men right to work building it. During the construction the head priest stirred up the neighbouring villagers and sent them to interfere with the work. In spite of this annoyance, the construction was completed.

No sooner had the fort been completed than wonderful news reached the Heroes of God. Bahá'u'lláh Himself would soon be arriving! Of those in the fort, only Mullá Ḥusayn had recognized that Bahá'u'lláh was the One for whom the Báb was preparing the way. He alone among the companions foresaw that it was Bahá'u'lláh Who would fulfil the Covenant of the Báb and complete His work. Excitedly, Mullá Ḥusayn made preparations to welcome His arrival. As soon as he saw Bahá'u'lláh coming he rushed forward, tenderly embraced Him and led Him to the place of honour he had prepared for Him. What indescribable joy filled the heart of Mullá Ḥusayn as he gazed upon Bahá'u'lláh! He stood speechless until at last Bahá'u'lláh asked that everyone be seated.

Bahá'u'lláh inspected the fortifications that had been built and said that they were satisfactory. He had but one suggestion, and that was that the one thing the fort and its company needed was the presence of Quddús.

He instructed Mullá Ḥusayn to send seven of his men to demand the release of Quddús, assuring him that they would be successful in their demands.

Bahá'u'lláh now gathered the companions together to bid them farewell. He told them of their obligation to be content with the will of God. He said to them, 'You have been chosen of God to be the vanguard of His host and the establishers of His Faith. His host verily will conquer. Whatever may befall, victory is yours, a victory which is complete and certain.'

With these words Bahá'u'lláh left those valiant Heroes to the care of God and departed. He had hoped to return to aid them, but unfortunately was arrested when attempting to return and join the defenders at the fort. But that is another story.

Mullá Ḥusayn immediately began to carry out the instructions of Bahá'u'lláh to free Quddús. He selected seven of his companions to go to the place where Quddús was being held and demand his release. This they did, and Quddús was set free. He headed straight for Fort Ṭabarsí to join Mullá Ḥusayn. Nearing the fort after darkness, he sent a messenger forward to tell of his coming. Upon hearing this news, Mullá Ḥusayn jumped to his feet with a burst of enthusiasm. The whole company arose with new courage and strength. Mullá Ḥusayn led about one hundred of them out to meet Quddús well before he arrived at the fort. In their hands he placed lighted candles, one in each hand, to light the way through the forest. As beautiful a light as it was, it could not compare to the light that shone in their hearts as they marched along.

Through the candlelit darkness they recognized, mounted upon a horse, the noble figure of Quddús. Pressing around his steed they looked up at the face they so longed to behold. Their words of devotion to him were proof of their undying love and loyalty. Still holding the lighted candles in their hands, they followed him on foot. Mullá Husayn began to sing and the others joined in. 'Holy, holy, the Lord our God, the Lord of the angels and spirit!' sang the voices of the companions around Quddús as they wound their way back through the forest night. What a lovely sight it was! – stars twinkling in the night sky above, candles flickering in the hands of the Heroes below, Quddús moving as a brilliant sun in their midst, and the voices of all raised in joy and praise of God!

When Quddús reached the fort, he fulfilled another of the events the keeper of the shrine had seen in his dream, that of the coming of the Prophet of God to the shrine. Dismounting from his horse, he leaned against the shrine and uttered the words the long-awaited Prophet was to say. Quddús could do this because the Báb had instructed him to act in His place as long as He was imprisoned. Mullá Husayn and his companions understood and accepted that Quddús was the greatest among them.

Now all was ready. With Quddús present, the company was complete. The fort was strongly built, and plenty of supplies were stored away. A few friendly people from nearby villages visited the fort and spread the word that it was a marvel to see. When this news reached the head priest of Barfurush, an uncontrollable jealousy filled his tormented soul. He sent a letter to the Shah begging him to send an army to destroy the followers of the Báb at the fort. He told the Shah that unless something was done about them they were going to take his kingdom from him. Unfortunately, the Shah believed this lie and commanded that an army be raised in the area and sent to destroy the Bábís at the fort.

In a short time an army of several thousand men was before the gates of Fort Ṭabarsí. Thus began the fulfilment of the third part of the dream of the keeper of the shrine, that of the heroic battles to be fought. The commander thought it would be an easy task for his great army to destroy the few hundred Bábís within the fort. Little did he understand the courage and strength of those whose hearts are filled with the love of God. His first order was to cut off the supply of food and water from nearby villagers to the fort. Next, he directed his men to build barricades before the fort, and ordered them to open fire on anyone who tried to leave. Standing atop the wall of the fort at sunset, Quddús and Mullá Ḥusayn surveyed the enemy gathered before them. Quddús mentioned that they were short of water, and that, God willing, a rainstorm would start, flood the enemy camp and relieve their own thirst. Furthermore, he hoped that it would be followed by snow, allowing them to drive away their assailants.

That very night a rainstorm hit, of such force that it flooded the enemy positions, soaking their gunpowder. At the same time, it delivered a large supply of water to the companions within the fort. This was followed the next night by a snowfall that further hampered the enemy. One of the companions exclaimed, 'Praise be to God, who has caused both rain and snow to fall upon our enemies; a fall that has brought desolation into their camp and refreshment into our fort.'

Despite these setbacks, the enemy continued preparations to attack. Quddús decided to charge out and scatter them before they could complete their preparations. Two hours after sunrise, Quddús, Mullá Ḥusayn and three others mounted their horses. With the entire company of their men following on foot behind, they flung open the gate of the fort, raised the call 'O Lord of the Age!' and charged out at the enemy. Caught by surprise, they scattered before the rush of the Heroes of God, leaving their belongings behind. Within a short span of time the commander, two of his officers and no fewer than 430 of their men lay sprawled, dead upon the ground. The dauntless Mullá Ḥusayn was still in hot pursuit when he got word from Quddús to return, saying, 'We need not carry further the punishment. Our purpose is to protect ourselves that we may be able to continue our labours for the regeneration of men. We have no intention whatever of causing unnecessary harm to anyone.'

Quddús ordered that nothing of the property of the enemy be taken, excepting horses and swords. With the enemy scattered for the time being, Quddús ordered that a moat be dug around the fort to give further protection against attack. No sooner had this work been completed than a new army commanded by a prince appeared upon the scene. Mullá Ḥusayn sent him messages asking for an opportunity to show the truth of the Revelation of the Báb, but never received a response. Soon it became clear that the Prince had come with the sole purpose of destroying the Bábís. His army of soldiers, horsemen and cannon assembled on a nearby hill, he gave the command to open fire in the direction of the fort. Meanwhile, he and his officers had set up headquarters in a fortified section of a nearby village.

'Mount your steeds, O heroes of God!' shouted Quddús. Mullá Ḥusayn and the men leaped upon their horses, the gates were flung open, and away they galloped toward the village where the enemy had set up camp. The hooves of their horses pounding across the mud and snow, they followed Quddús. They were met by a hail of bullets as they approached the enemy camp. Ignoring the danger, they charged straight for the stronghold of the enemy. Mullá Ḥusayn leading the way, he forced his way through the gates and charged into the private room of the Prince. Fearing for his life, the Prince jumped out of a back window, running for safety in his bare feet. This show of cowardice by the Prince gave the signal for the rest to flee in panic before the little band of Heroes. Of the riches the Prince had left behind, Mullá Ḥusayn took only his sword as proof of their victory. They remained the rest of the night in the area to see what the enemy would do next.

As the sun rose, the victors gathered to observe the movements of the scattered enemy. Seeing them prepare to counter-attack, Mullá Ḥusayn ordered the men to protect Quddús while he kept watch from a good distance. The enemy divided and attacked Quddús and his men in one direction and Mullá Ḥusayn in the other. Mullá Ḥusayn turned to face the attack from his position, and Quddús and the men from theirs. Fearing the mighty Mullá Ḥusayn, the enemy charging toward him swerved away and joined the others in the attack upon Quddús, surrounding him. They took aim and fired a volley of bullets into their midst. One bullet struck Quddús in the mouth, seriously injuring him.

Mullá Ḥusayn came galloping to the rescue. Horrified at the sight of what had happened, he jumped from his horse and ran to the side of Quddús. The sight of blood dripping from the mouth of his leader angered and grieved him; Quddús saw his distress and commanded him to calm himself and take no account of this injury; the enemy were closing in from all sides as they spoke. Mullá Ḥusayn saw that he had to act quickly to avoid disaster. Taking the sword of the wounded Quddús in one hand and with the captured sword of the Prince in the other, he turned to face the enemy surrounding them. What steel-like determination must have flashed from his eyes! What fear must have gripped the hearts of the enemy at the approach of the fearless Mullá Ḥusayn, a noble blade in each hand! With power and agility the matchless hero strode forward, those dreaded blades whirring in the air, cutting down foes like so many trees before him. As before, the awesome might of Mullá Ḥusayn and his men gained the day, sending the remaining enemy in retreat, but at an awful cost: the wounding of their leader, Quddús!

Gathering themselves together, the companions made their way back to the fort. Seeing the sadness of his companions because of his injury, Quddús consoled them by writing these words, 'Though my body be afflicted, my soul is immersed in gladness. My gratitude to God knows no bounds. If you love me, suffer not that this joy be obscured by the sight of your lamentations.'

One report tells how, at some point in the conflict, Mullá Ḥusayn addressed the gathered enemy soldiers in much the same way as the Imam Husayn had done over a thousand years before. With these words he reminded them of his innocence and that of his companions: 'O people, why do ye act so cruelly towards us and strive without cause to shed innocent blood?' Some hearts of the enemy were moved, as in the days of the Imam Husayn. Seeing this, the Captain fired his gun and ordered his soldiers to shout so as to drown out the voice of Mullá Ḥusayn. Mullá Ḥusayn, so the story goes, then called out three times, 'Is there anyone who will help me?' The soldiers became silent. Tears began to flow down some of their faces. The lines of horsemen began to move uneasy in their places. The Captain saw that unless he did something quickly, the whole army might go over to Mullá Ḥusayn's side, so he ordered them to begin firing. Seeing that they would not listen, Mullá Ḥusayn drew his sword, raised his voice to heaven and called out, 'O God, I have completed the proof to this host, but it availeth not.' Once again he attacked them on the right and on the left.

A lull in the months-long battle was broken when the army of the Prince received reinforcements. After setting up camp, he ordered that seven barricades be built around the fort, from which they planned to launch their attack against Mullá Ḥusayn and his men. This work completed, his troops began marching to and fro performing military drills to frighten the defenders within the walls of the fort. Unimpressed by this show, the companions inside began to dig a well, their supply of water having run low.

(This brings this history to the point in time recounted in Chapter 1.)

Mullá Ḥusayn knew that the time for his glorious death was near. Gazing upon the men at work, he remarked, 'Today we shall have all the water we require for our bath. Cleansed of all earthly defilements, we shall seek the court of the Almighty and shall hasten to our eternal abode . . . This night, ere the hour of dawn, let those who wish to join me be ready to issue forth from behind these walls and, scattering once again the dark forces which have beset our path, ascend . . . to the heights of glory.'

That afternoon he said his prayers and began to prepare himself for his last battle. He spoke with the men, cheering them with indescribable joy upon his face. Then he went to be alone with Quddús. Sitting at the feet of Quddús, who so powerfully reminded him of his Beloved, the Báb, he poured out to him the secrets of his soul.

Now he was ready for his last and most unforgettable battle for the emancipation of his Faith. After midnight he gazed up at the morning star. He knew it was a sign of his reunion with his Beloved in the world above. The green turban the Báb had given him was upon his head as he mounted his charger. The call of, 'O Lord of the Age!' echoed across the field of battle. The force of his charge scattered the enemy, but before the victory was complete, a rifleman's shot felled the inspired hero. In the darkness and confusion, the man did not know whom his shot had hit.

Two companions came to Mullá Ḥusayn's rescue and carried the mortally wounded warrior back to the fort. Arriving safely, they laid the life-stricken Mullá Ḥusayn before Quddús. He called his name and Mullá Ḥusayn rose and knelt before him. He lived long enough to hear these words from Quddús, 'You have hastened the hour of your departure, and have abandoned me to my foes. Please God, I will ere long join you and taste the sweetness of heaven's ineffable delights.' Then Mullá Ḥusayn asked him, 'May my life be a ransom for you. Are you well pleased with me?'

And so the final scene from the dream of the keeper of the shrine was fulfilled, as Mullá Ḥusayn had said it would. The matchless warrior of God, the Gate of the Gate of God, the first to believe, the mighty Mullá Ḥusayn, passed from this sad world into the Celestial City of never-failing joy and brightness. Souls such as him are willing to sacrifice their earthly lives because they are certain that a greater life awaits them after death.

Quddús directed that his body and those of his companions killed in the battle be buried in separate graves near the Shrine of S͟hayk͟h Ṭabarsí. Gazing upon the fresh graves of the fallen Heroes of God, Quddús remarked,

'Let the loved ones of God take heed of the example of these martyrs of our Faith. Let them in life be and remain as united as these are now in death.'

It took forty-five days for the enemy to recover from the damage they had received at the hand of Mullá Ḥusayn. Yet they were alert enough to prevent any supplies or reinforcements from entering the fort.

In the meantime, Quddús took an important step. Because of the loss of Mullá Ḥusayn he had to choose another of the companions to act as his second-in-command. The man he chose, called Muḥammad-Báqir, was well known to him and had served him devotedly before joining Mullá Ḥusayn's attempt to rescue him. He would rank seventh on the list of martyrs, but not until he carried out three astounding acts of heroism.

With supplies running dangerously low, Quddús felt he should warn the remaining companions of the intense suffering and devastation that would soon be upon them. He invited those with the least trace of fear to escape now, before the way be closed forever. On hearing this warning, one coward amongst them decided to betray Quddús and his gallant band of men. He sent a secret message to the enemy commander telling him of the death of Mullá Ḥusayn, and that the Bábís were worn down because of the lack of food and losses in battle.

This was the best news the commander could hear. The death of Mullá Ḥusayn, he mistakenly thought, removed the only barrier preventing his victory over the Bábís and the restoration of his reputation. Determined to get full credit for defeating the Bábís, he killed the messenger on the spot so that none could suspect the true reason for his boldness and expected victory. With mistaken confidence he gave orders to prepare to renew the attack. Proudly marching with his banner at the head of his troops, he surrounded the fort and gave the order to open fire.

Inside, Quddús summoned Muḥammad-Báqir. He instructed him to choose eighteen of his companions and go out and give the enemy the punishment they deserved for their aggression. 'Let him realize', he said, 'that though Mullá Ḥusayn be no more, God's invincible power still continues to sustain his companions.'

Once again the gates were flung open, and once again the cries of, 'Mount your steeds, O heroes of God!' and 'O Lord of the Age!' were sounded. The big horses snorted, pawed the air and charged pell-mell at the enemy. Like an avenging wind of God, Muḥammad-Báqir and his men stormed onto the field of battle. The sound of their thundering hooves and the awesome sight of the warriors with their swords raised on high struck such fear into the hearts of the enemy that they turned and fled in terror. Forward thundered the Heroes of God, their blades seldom missing their mark. Only a few of the enemy escaped with their lives. The terrified commander deserted his flag, fell from his horse, and, leaving one boot dangling from its stirrup, beat a hasty retreat in the direction his men had taken. Shamefaced, he returned to confess his defeat to the Prince. On prancing horses the victors returned to the fort, and Muḥammad-Báqir presented the deserted flag to Quddús, as a sign of their victory.

This victory gave the companions a rest for a while,

but it was an uneasy rest, for their food was running out. The situation was so bad that they had to eat the meat of horses they had captured from the enemy, but in spite of the gnawing hunger, their spirits were raised by the prayers and songs they sang in praise of God.

Reeling from the wreckage left by Muḥammad-Báqir, the Prince realized he needed more fire-power if he were to defeat such a brave people as the Bábís. He demanded that bomb-shells and cannons with fresh reinforcements be sent to him from the capital. As the big guns arrived and were wheeled into place, Quddús and his men prepared to celebrate Naw-Rúz inside the fort. Ignoring both the danger outside and their own hunger, they celebrated the New Year with joy and thanksgiving. For a number of days and nights their voices were raised to heaven with the verse, 'Holy, holy, the Lord our God, the Lord of the angels and the spirit.'

On the ninth day after Naw-Rúz, the Prince gave the order that the bombardment of the fort begin. As the cannonballs began to fall, Quddús walked to the centre of the fort. Suddenly a cannonball, flying over the wall, landed at his feet. Calmly, he rolled it back and forth under his foot. Addressing his companions, he noted how unaware these aggressors were of the power of God's wrath. He reminded them that they were the blessed companions of God in this day, and that only the thought of self could rob them of this honour. He told them never to fear the threats of the wicked, for no one could alter their allotted span of life. He ended with these words, 'Should you allow your hearts to be agitated for but one moment by the booming of these guns which, with increasing violence, will continue to shower their shot upon this fort, you will have cast yourselves out of the stronghold of Divine protection.'

Continuing the bombardment without interruption for several days, the Prince had hoped for the unconditional surrender of the defenders of the fort. A few of the faint-hearted, shaking with fear, huddled together in a sheltered corner of the fort, their eyes fixed upon the fearless, God-filled companions. As much as they wished, they could not overcome their fear. The gnawing hunger, endless bombardment and threat of death were more than they could bear, while from the Heroes was heard an unending chorus of hymns and thanksgiving.

Completely frustrated by the unbreakable spirit of Quddús and his companions, the enemy built a tower from which they hoped the cannon-fire would have more effect. Observing this, Quddús called forward his valiant lieutenant, Muḥammad-Báqir. He instructed him to go with his eighteen men and punish the enemy as they had done before. He sent him on his mission with these words, 'Let him know that God's lion-hearted warriors, when pressed and driven by hunger, are able to manifest deeds of such heroism as no ordinary mortals can show.'

Open swung the gates, 'O Lord of the Age!' shouted Muḥammad-Báqir and his men, forward thundered the Heroes of God. Fighting their way to the tower, the fearless companions laid thirty soldiers and their officer dead in the dust. Storming up one side of it, they captured the guns and threw them to the ground. Next, they demolished as many of the defences as the remaining daylight would allow. Gathering together some of the fattest horses the scattered enemy had left behind, they returned in triumph to the fort.

The damage from this attack, combined with an explosion of the enemy's ammunition dump which killed a number of men and officers, prevented the Prince from attacking for a whole month. During this time the Bábís feasted on the horses until the last of them were eaten. And once again hunger began to have its effect on them. It became so bad they were forced to eat the leather of their shoes. Nevertheless, the Heroes, led again by the stout-hearted Muḥammad-Báqir, were able to repel another attack by the enemy with the same victorious results.

At this point the Prince became desperate. Everything he had tried had ended in total defeat. After eleven months of battle his grand army had failed; not only failed to defeat a few hundred Bábís, but failed to even begin to break their spirit. He ordered a pause in the assault while he figured out what next to do. He decided to use treachery on Quddús and his companions. This was his shameful plan: he would call a truce, and then swear on his Holy Qur'án and in the name of God that Quddús and the rest of the Bábís could pass from the fort in safety. Then, when the Bábís thought they were safe, he would divide and disarm them, and do with them as he wished. When the offer was presented to Quddús, he replied that God would decide between them, and that he would allow them to demonstrate the sincerity of their intentions by accepting the offer.

Now the depth of evil deceit in the Prince showed itself. When the companions left the fort they were treated kindly, until, by means of a lie, they were separated. One group was seized and sold into slavery. Some were shot, speared, or chopped to pieces. Others were tied to trees and riddled with bullets. Sadistically, some were placed in front of the barrels of cannons, and then blown to bits. The heads of the gallant Bábí captains Muḥammad-Báqir and Muḥammad-Taqí were carried on the ends of spears to Barfurush. Although the hands of the Prince were dripping with the innocent blood of the Heroes of God, his treachery was not yet over.

Now, only Quddús was left. The Prince hesitated to go so far as to stain his hand with the sacred blood of Quddús. He decided to take him to the town of Barfurush, where the drama had begun, to celebrate the destruction of the Bábís. After three days of merry-making, he thought to take Quddús as his prisoner to the capital to show the King. He might have done this, too, had it not been for one person – the cowardly, insanely jealous, mad priest of Barfurush.

He was the same one who had stirred up hatred and spread lies about the Bábís in the first place. He could not bear the idea of Quddús passing out of his clutches, so he used every devilish trick to get Quddús into his own hands. To his crooked mind, killing Quddús would be a great source of pleasure. Using his same method as before, he called the townspeople together. He ranted and raved against Quddús until they were a lawless, murderous mob, screaming for his life.

The Prince decided to have a hearing between the priests of the town and Quddús. Everyone gathered for the meeting, and when Quddús defended himself with convincing truth, the head priest fell into a rage. Throwing his turban to the ground, he stormed out of the room complaining that soon Quddús would have them all convinced that he was the mouthpiece of God. At this point, the Prince released Quddús into the hands of the priests. 'I wash my hands of all responsibility for any harm that may befall this man,' he then said, so reminiscent of the words of Pontius Pilate about Jesus Christ, 'You are free to do what you like with him.' His dastardly deeds finished, the Prince mounted his horse and rode away, turning his back on Quddús and fixing shame to his name forever after.

As soon as the Prince was gone the sadistic head priest began to gratify his foul, fiendish desires. What tortures he dreamt up! Quddús was forced to walk a path of pain that no pen can adequately describe. Bahá'u'lláh Himself has testified that the holy Quddús, at the bloom of his youth, endured more torture and suffered a death more awful than that of Jesus Christ at the hour of His greatest agony!

Stripped and loaded with chains, Quddús was paraded through the streets of Barfurush. Each step of the way a fresh blow was dealt to his youthful body. Each step of the way a new torment was heaped upon him. Each step of the way the women rabble of the city cursed and spit upon him. Beaten, stabbed and desecrated, he was driven onward. At one stage a man who had abandoned

Quddús from the fort and gone over to the side of the governor approached him and slapped him in the face. Ridiculing him, he asked Quddús why he did not save himself, since he claimed that his voice was the voice of God? Looking his tormentor directly in the eye, Quddús asked that God forgive him for what he had done. Blood pouring from his many wounds, his life was draining away; but his spirit was eternally strong.

In the midst of his agony, just before he died Quddús whispered these words, 'Forgive, O my God, the trespasses of this people. Deal with them in Thy mercy . . . Show them, O God, the way of Truth, and turn their ignorance into faith.'

Then, his mortal body finished, the bloodthirsty mob chopped his body into pieces, and cast the parts into a fire.

Thus ended the earthly life of the noble Quddús. But those flames that consumed his flesh did not end the story of this glorious martyr and his companions, they only heralded its beginning. Even now, it is being told and retold around firesides in the farthest corners of the world. And this shall continue until it becomes the heritage of all peoples, when, generation after generation, the flame of love for Quddús, Mullá Husayn and their faithful companions is kindled in the heart of man.

CHAPTER SIX

THE SEVEN HEROES OF GOD AT TEHRAN

Throughout the whole time of the struggle at Fort Ṭabarsí, the imprisoned Báb anxiously awaited word of the fate of the defenders. When the awful news of what had happened reached Him His heart was crushed with grief. His moans of sadness and weeping prevented Him from eating for nine whole days. Sunk in a sea of sorrow for five months, not a word flowed from His pen. Tears raining from His eyes, He sat alone in His cell communing with His Beloved. At last His pain subsided enough for Him to write again; streams of verses began to flow in praise of the twin Heroes, Quddús and Mullá Ḥusayn.

When he had finished these Tablets, He called a believer to Him who had been serving as His attendant in the prison. Entrusting into his hands specific Tablets He had revealed in honour of the martyrs of Ṭabarsí, He assigned to him the mission to visit the scene of the battles. 'Arise,' said the Báb, 'and with complete detachment . . . visit, on My behalf, the spot which enshrines the bodies of those immortals who, with their blood, have sealed their faith in My Cause. As you approach the precincts of that hallowed ground, put off your shoes and, bowing your head in reverence to their memory, invoke their names and prayerfully make the circuit of their shrine. Bring back to Me, as a remembrance of your visit, a handful of that holy earth which covers the remains of My beloved ones, Quddús and Mullá Ḥusayn.' Faithfully, his attendant carried out every detail of this mission.

Meanwhile, in the capital city of Tehran, suspicion and hatred of the Bábís continued to spread. The Shah gave his chief minister, the Grand Vizier, permission to deal with the Bábís in any way he saw fit. This Grand Vizier hated the Bábís nearly as much as did the head priest of Barfurush. His fear, which was completely unfounded, was that they might overthrow the government.

Fourteen Bábís had been arrested and brought to a house to force them to tell of their activities. They were tortured in every way one could imagine, but they refused to talk. One, by the name of Muḥammad-Ḥusayn, was put to unusually extreme kinds of torture, but never uttered a word. His tormenters wondered if he was a mute. They asked Mullá Ismá'íl, who had converted him to his Faith, if he was able to speak at all. Mullá Ismá'íl answered that he was perfectly able to speak. He then turned to him and called his name. Muḥammad-Ḥusayn instantly answered his teacher. Frustrated with the Bábís' refusal to cooperate, the tormentors appealed to the Grand Vizier of the Shah for help.

Appearing personally at the scene, the Grand Vizier gave the order that the penalty for any of them who refused to deny his belief in the Báb would be death. This was the final test of their faith. Seven of the prisoners, the tortures and threat of death too much for them, denied their faith and were set free; their belief in the Báb simply was not strong enough. The remaining seven chose death rather than deny their faith, and in so doing, fixed their stars in the constellation of the immortal Heroes of the new Age.

The first to fall was the uncle of the Báb, Ḥájí Mírzá Siyyid 'Alí. He had lovingly cared for the Báb and had been the first to believe in the city of Shiraz. The Grand Vizier told him that some of the wealthy merchants had offered to buy his freedom, but he would have none of it. The Vizier tempted him with promises of freedom and honour if he would utter but one word of denial. His answer was that if he were to deny the truth of his kinsman, the Báb, he would have to deny Moses, Jesus, Muhammad and every other prophet who came before them. 'God knows', he added, 'that whatever I have heard and read concerning the sayings and doings of those Messengers, I have been privileged to witness the same from this Youth, this beloved Kinsman of mine, from His earliest boyhood to this, the thirtieth year of His life . . . I only request of you that you allow me to be the first to lay down my life in the path of my beloved Kinsman.'

The Grand Vizier was struck dumb by this answer. Without uttering a single word, he motioned that the uncle of the Báb be taken to the public square and be beheaded. As the prisoner was led to the place of execution a crowd gathered to witness the awful sight. A public execution was something new to them, because up to this time the custom had been to kill the doomed in front of the Shah in his private room. Morbid curiosity attracted a huge crowd to see the horrid spectacle. Facing them, he cried: 'Hear me, O people, I have offered up myself as a willing sacrifice in the path of the Cause of God.' He went on to remind them that it was well known that he was not guilty of any crime, and that the Báb was the very One for whom they all had been hoping and praying. He prayed that God forgive them for their blindness, and that their eyes be opened to the truth of the new Day of God. These words stirred his executioner to the depths of his soul. Pretending that his sword needed sharpening, he left the scene, determined not to return. Nevertheless, the horrible task was finished by another executioner.

The next to fall was a man by the name of Mírzá Qurbán-'Alí. He was widely known for his sterling character and saintliness. Many people searched him out to pay their respects and enjoy the benefit of his company, for they considered him a man of God. The news of his arrest accounted, in part, for the large crowds who had gathered to learn of the proceedings. Having learned of the Cause of the Báb from Mullá Ḥusayn, he was greatly disappointed that an illness had prevented him from joining the Heroes at Fort Ṭabarsí and dying a martyr's death with them. He looked upon this challenge as an opportunity to make up for this failure.

The Grand Vizier told him of the numerous admirers who had gathered to plea for his release. Qurbán-'Alí told him that though he might have a thousand admirers, he did not have the power to change the heart of a single one of them, whereas the Báb had the power to change the souls of the worst of men. The Grand Vizier said that he did not want to condemn to death such an important man as he. 'Why hesitate,' Qurbán-'Alí impatiently interrupted, '. . . rest assured that I shall never blame you for your act. The sooner you strike off my head, the greater will be my gratitude to you.'

'Take him away from this place!', cried the Vizier, afraid that he himself should fall under his spell. Qurbán-'Alí replied that the Vizier need not worry about that happening, for his kind could never be made to understand the entrancing Divine power which transforms the souls of men. Enraged with this reply, the Grand Vizier rose from his seat, and, his whole body shaking with anger, shouted: 'Nothing but the edge of a sword can silence the voice of this deluded people!' Turning to the executioners standing nearby, he exclaimed: 'No need to bring any more members of this hateful sect before me . . . Whomever you are able to induce to recant his faith, release him; as for the rest, strike off their heads.'

As Qurbán-'Alí was led to the square by the executioners, his voice sang out with delight, 'Hasten to slay me, for through this death you will have offered me the chalice of everlasting life.' Turning to the crowd, he gave testimony to the Cause of God, and pleaded that they take heed, and recognize the dawn of the Day of God. Seeing how deaf the people were to his call, he lamented that he could find no one with whom he could share the joy of his sacrifice.

At the sight of the body of the Báb's uncle, headless and bleeding at his feet, Qurbán-'Alí realized that he was the friend with whom he was to share this moment of supreme sacrifice. Flinging himself upon the body, he shouted: 'Hail, hail the day of mutual rejoicing, the day of our reunion with our Beloved!' Taking the body up into his arms, he could feel that its spirit yet remained; he sensed that it was waiting, so that they could leave this world together. Excitedly, he called to his executioner: 'Approach and strike your blow, for my faithful comrade is unwilling to release himself from my embrace, and calls me to hasten together with him to the court of the Well-Beloved.' Down fell the sword on the back of his neck. And so, together, the twin souls of Ḥájí Mírzá Siyyid 'Alí and Mírzá Qurbán-'Alí winged their way to the world beyond.

Then came the turn of Ḥájí Mullá Ismá'íl-i-Qumí. He had attended the Conference of Badasht, where Bahá'u'lláh gave him the title 'Mystery of Being'. When he saw lying before him the headless bodies of his companions, locked in each other's arms and their gory heads along the side, he cried, 'Well done beloved companions!' Facing his executioner, he said, 'I have forgiven you your act; approach and deal your blow.' Then he looked to heaven and cried, 'Accept me, O my God, unworthy though I be, and deign to inscribe my name upon the scroll of those immortals who have laid down their lives on the altar of sacrifice.' His lips were still moving in prayer when the sword fell. He too had refused to say those five little words: 'I am not a Bábí.'

Next to be brought to the chopping block was a man by the name of Siyyid Ḥusayn. Standing before the crowd he reminded them that he was a descendant of the Imam Husayn. He called to their attention the fact that he was recognized as an expert on the law and teachings of Islam, and that with this knowledge he could prove the truth of the Message brought by the Báb. Not willing to listen, an officer of the Grand Vizier interrupted and stabbed him to death on the spot.

The remaining three, as the events unfolded, would be martyred together. Ḥájí Muḥammad-Taqí was led out. The ghastly sight of his beloved companions angered him. He was especially moved at the sight of Siyyid Ḥusayn, for he it was who had taught him the Cause of the Báb. He turned to his tormentor and burst out these words: 'Approach, you wretched and heartless tyrant, and hasten to slay me, for I am impatient to join my beloved Ḥusayn. To live after him is a torture I cannot endure.'

At this moment the next in line, Siyyid Murtaḍá, threw himself forward insisting that he be allowed to be martyred next. Then Muḥammad-Ḥusayn, who had silently endured the tortures, rushed out and begged that he be martyred before either of them. Their eagerness to go one before the other astounded the onlookers. Everyone wondered which of the three companions would go next to the block. They pleaded with such eagerness that it was decided to behead them together and at the same time. And it was done.

Picture, if you can, the final scene in your mind. See the crowd standing in wide-eyed shock, some sick with sorrow and others filled with twisted delight. See the seven bodies, six of them headless, lying here and there in the bloody gore of death. See the cruel executioner and officers standing over them, spattered with the sacred blood of the fallen Heroes. And see, rising above the sad spectacle, the hallowed souls of the seven martyrs returning to their Creator.

It was over. And we are stirred to the depths of our souls to see so great a faith stand so fast before such cruelty, a faith so great that it won for the Seven Martyrs of Tehran a place forever among the Heroes of God.

CHAPTER SEVEN

VAḤÍD
HERO OF GOD AT NAYRÍZ

Vaḥíd was the man sent by the Shah to investigate the Báb, and, who, during the course of that interview, became His devoted servant forever. Vaḥíd never returned to report to the Shah. From that moment on he decided to spend his last ounce of energy spreading the news of the coming of the 'Lord of the Age', whom he knew the Báb to be. He was travelling from town to town when he heard of the battle that was raging at Fort Ṭabarsí.

He headed immediately for Tehran to prepare to join Mullá Ḥusayn at the Fort. Everything ready, he was about to leave when Bahá'u'lláh arrived and told him it would be hopeless to try and join them. He was upset and disappointed at this news, but the companionship of Bahá'u'lláh was an unexpected pleasure, and he visited Him often. This was a wonderful opportunity to absorb the matchless wisdom that only He possessed.

One evening was especially memorable. Some of the believers were gathered at the home of Bahá'u'lláh. Ṭáhirih and Vaḥíd were both present, and so was 'Abdu'l-Bahá, the young son of Bahá'u'lláh. Ṭáhirih held 'Abdu'l-Bahá upon her knee as she listened to a conversation between

Vaḥíd and Bahá'u'lláh. Vaḥíd was giving endless expla-
nations of the truth of the Báb's mission. She spoke up, as
'Abdu'l-Bahá, perched upon her knee, listened excitedly.
In her musical, golden-toned voice she told Vaḥíd that the
time for talk was over; what was needed now was action!
These words must have had their intended effect, for it
was not long before the tireless Vaḥíd was once again on
the road travelling city to city teaching the Cause of God.

In time his travels brought him back to his beautiful
home in the city of Yazd. It was the season of Naw-Rúz,
so he was happy to join his wife and sons as well as his
friends. He was one of the most prominent persons of the
town, so when he arrived all the important priests and
city officials came to greet him and celebrate the New
Year. Vaḥíd thought this was an ideal opportunity to proclaim the truth of his new Faith. Holding nothing back,
he explained the principles and demonstrated the truth
of the cause of the Báb.

When he had finished, the listeners had divided into
two groups: those whose hearts were ready to receive
the new Word of God, and those whose hearts were so
hardened they only hated him for what he had said. The
latter group were those who had always secretly been
jealous of Vaḥíd. They seized this opportunity to bring
him down, claiming that he would soon wreck the religion of their forefathers. Their leader was a man known
as the Navváb.

The news of what had happened at the meeting spread
like wildfire throughout the district. It had a strange effect
on the people; they were either attracted or repelled;

either the flame of hate or of hope was ignited in the heart of each who heard the extraordinary claim of Vaḥíd. For forty days and forty nights his house was the centre for study and teaching of the Faith of the Báb. All this activity gave an excuse to the Navváb to spread suspicion of the followers of Vaḥíd and his new religion. Like the mad priest of Barfurush, he could never rest until the followers of the Báb were all killed.

The love that people had for Vaḥíd and his fame further aroused the jealousy of the Navváb. Plotting ways in which to destroy Vaḥíd, he went to the governor of the city and did all he could to scare him into taking action against Vaḥíd and his hated followers. Young and inexperienced, the governor was already nervous because rebels had been terrorizing the area recently. Apparently he did not know that these rebels had no connection with the Bábí religion. Acting hastily, he sent a group of armed men to attack the house of Vaḥíd. Meanwhile, the insanely jealous Navváb got together the riff-raff of the streets and sent them to join in the attack.

Vaḥíd's companions became alarmed when soldiers and an angry mob appeared outside the house. Anxiously, they turned to Vaḥíd and asked what they should do. He was as calm as a man could be, hardly paying any attention to the commotion outside. He told them that they could rest at ease because God, the all-powerful Avenger, would crush their foe this night.

The leader of a group of the town ruffians had defied successive local governors. This rebellious man was Muḥammad-'Abdu'lláh. A rumour had spread that he was dead, but actually he was in hiding with his band of men in the mountains. When word of the new Faith of God reached him, he accepted it completely. Hearing trouble was brewing for the Bábís at the home of Vaḥíd, he decided the time was right to reappear.

Riding out of the night at the head of his band of men, he must have appeared as an avenging angel of God returned from the dead. Raising the battle cry 'O Lord of the Age!' Muḥammad-'Abdu'lláh led the charge into the midst of the enemy gathered at Vaḥíd's house. Caught by complete surprise, they threw down their weapons and ran for their lives. Together with the governor they escaped to a nearby stronghold.

The rebel-turned-hero then asked to be introduced to Vaḥíd. He assured Vaḥíd of his allegiance to the Cause of the Báb, and then asked what plans he had made to destroy their enemy. Vaḥíd had no such plans. He advised him to leave the city and trust the outcome to God. The rough-and-ready former rebel replied that he could never abandon his friends to the mercy of a murderous enemy. If he did so, he asked, what would be the difference between him and those who abandoned the Imam Husayn at Karbila in a former age? Then he said: 'A merciful God will, I trust, be indulgent towards me and will forgive my action.' The discussion ended, Muḥammad-'Abdu'lláh rode off with his men to deal with the enemy in a manner he felt they deserved. Spurring on his horse, he headed toward the stronghold of the governor.

Meanwhile, the jealousy-crazed Navváb did what he could to stir up the townspeople to take action against

Vaḥíd. Vaḥíd, doing what he could to avoid a confrontation, sent one of the most courageous of the Bábís, named Siyyid-i-Khál-Dár, to ride through the town inviting the people to join the Cause of the Lord of the Age, the Báb. His voice thundering through the streets, he also warned them that the Bábís would defend themselves if they were not left in peace. Frightened by such boldness, the people said they would do nothing to disturb Vaḥíd.

This refusal to fight against Vaḥíd blocked the evil intentions of the Navváb for the time being. Nevertheless, he talked a number of people into turning their wrath against Muḥammad-'Abdu'lláh who had taken up a position before the stronghold of the governor. When the governor saw help arriving from the town, he ordered his men to come out of their cover and join in the fight against Muḥammad-'Abdu'lláh. In the clash that followed Muḥammad-'Abdu'lláh was shot in the foot and thrown to the ground. He had his brother carry him to the house of Vaḥíd.

The emboldened enemy followed him there, hoping to finish him off. Hearing the clamour outside, Vaḥíd sent out seven of his companions to drive them away, which they did. When the dust had settled, they found the wounded Muḥammad-'Abdu'lláh lying in front of the house. He recovered from his wound, but was eventually slain by the enemy.

Calling everyone together that night, Vaḥíd told them to disperse quietly in separate directions. He asked his wife to take their two youngest children to the home of her father, where they would be safe. The two eldest sons he would take with him. All else, his belongings, his beautiful house and its furnishings, were to be forgotten. He said that he had accumulated these fabulous possessions for the sole purpose of sacrificing them in the path of God. His earnest hope was that this sacrifice would open the eyes of these faithless people to what he had found, the Pearl of Greatest Price, the Báb. As soon as the townspeople realized he had left, they looted the house and tore it to the ground.

Vaḥíd selected two hearty men to accompany him and his sons on their journey, the destination of which was his home in Nayríz. One of the men, Ghulám-Riḍá, was to play a key role in the heroic battles to come. Although the enemy were hot on their trail, they made their escape safely through the mountains. Vaḥíd offered his new-found Faith to every soul he met along the way.

Though the journey took Vaḥíd through very rough country, he showed no signs of tiring. No sooner did he enter a village than he would go to the mosque, have the people called, and teach the Cause of God. Great numbers were moved by his words and accepted the religion of the Báb. If none responded to His call, he would straightaway march out of the village. He was seeking souls who could carry on the work when he left.

His travels finally brought him to the outskirts of Nayríz. The news of his coming had reached the town before him, so a large group of people were waiting to greet him when he arrived.

The governor of Nayríz had a tremendous fear of Vaḥíd and his new Faith. He threatened those who went to meet Vaḥíd with punishment and even death unless they returned. This order had absolutely no effect on them, on the contrary, they became even more attached to Vaḥíd than before. The governor could hardly believe such disobedience to his wishes. Aware that the governor might turn the people against him, Vaḥíd made plans to move to his home village where the people were more friendly and a strong fort was close by where he could go if he needed protection against an attack.

In the meantime, Vaḥíd proceeded to the town of Nayríz itself. He was so eager to address the multitudes who had gathered to hear him that he did not bother to go to his house. Covered with dust from the road he entered the mosque, climbed the pulpit and cast his eyes upon no fewer than fifteen hundred persons gathered to hear him.

He spoke with such power and conviction that every soul present was electrified. The adoring crowd began to surge forward. Unable to contain their love and gratitude, they cried out enthusiastically: 'We have heard and we obey! We have heard and we obey!' The spell his words cast upon their hearts was such as had never before been heard in Nayríz.

After they had calmed themselves, Vaḥíd explained why he had come. 'My sole purpose', he said, 'in coming to Nayríz is to proclaim the Cause of God. I thank and glorify Him for having enabled me to touch your hearts with His Message.'

Then he begged them to permit him to leave, for he wanted no harm to come to them from the governor on his account. But they insisted that he stay awhile longer, and as for the hardships this should entail, with one voice they answered: 'We are ready and resigned to the will of God. God grant us His grace to withstand the calamities that may yet befall us.'

It was settled. The men and women pressed around him in wild excitement; cheering all the while, they joined hands and escorted him home.

This evidence of the loyalty of the people to Vaḥíd reawakened the hatred of the governor. Convinced that this new religion would undermine his own authority, he gave orders that an army be raised to destroy it once and for all. He got together a well-trained and equipped army of about one thousand men, consisting of both foot soldiers and horsemen. His plan was to attack suddenly and take Vaḥíd prisoner.

Vaḥíd got wind of his plan and decided to take measures to defend himself. He sent twenty men to an abandoned and dilapidated fort outside of town, called Fort Khájih. Their instructions were to repair and fortify the stronghold. In the meantime, the governor had moved back to the main part of town. Forcing one of the Bábís out of his own house, he sent marksmen to the roof and they opened fire, wounding an old man saying his prayers on a rooftop nearby. He was the first Bábí victim of Nayríz.

As soon as Vaḥíd learned of this attack, he arose early the next morning, mounted his horse, and with a number of his companions rode to Fort Khájih, where they could better defend themselves. This brought the total of Bábí defenders to seventy-two, the same number of armed men who had stood with the Imam Husayn so long ago.

The governor took immediate action. He sent his brother at the head of the force one thousand strong with orders to attack the fort. The invaders had barely arrived when a stout-hearted band of Bábí defenders charged out and easily chased them away.

The news of the defeat of the governor's men reached the ears of a powerful prince in the city of Shiraz. He ordered the governor to exterminate everyone in the fort. Vahíd sent warning to the governor that he would receive a punishing defeat if he continued his aggression against them. When the governor ignored this warning, Vahíd sent a group of young men, inexperienced in the ways of war but of magnificent courage, against the oppressors. The enemy withered away before their awesome charge, and the brother of the governor was killed in the retreat. Completely disgraced, the governor sent a request to the Prince, begging him to send reinforcements and heavy cannons.

Vahíd knew that it was to be a life or death struggle from this point forward. While the Prince considered the request of the governor, Vahíd organized the men in the fort into a smooth-working, fighting force. The work was divided and officers were chosen. Ghulám-Ridá, who had accompanied him and his sons on the journey to Nayríz, was to be captain. The governor decided to appeal again to the Prince to send the help he needed, but this time he enclosed a 'gift' of a great deal of money. The messenger was intercepted along the way and brought to Vahíd, to whom he confessed the details of his mission. Vahíd was willing to forgive him, yet the companions eventually put him to death because of his hatred for Vaḥíd.

Hoping to get the help he needed, the governor sent a troop of men loaded with gifts to the Prince. In addition, he wrote letters to powerful priests in Shiraz alarming them with lies about the intentions of Vaḥíd. He urged them to get the Prince to take action.

At last the Prince agreed to help. He raised a large army equipped with cannons to join in the battle against the Bábís. Surrounding the fort, they dug trenches, built barricades, set up the big guns and opened fire. A Bábí sharpshooter in the fort took careful aim at the captain directing the cannon-fire and dropped him with one shot. The enemy dove for their trenches, and the guns went silent.

Everything was quiet until the next night, when the enemy renewed the bombardment. Vaḥíd instructed his captain, Ghulám-Riḍá, to choose fourteen companions and drive off the enemy. Those he selected were mostly old men, one of whom was a shoemaker more than ninety years of age! The remainder were mere boys. Who could believe that such a group would be capable of such a task? But this did not matter, for the Heroes of God, whoever they may be, are transformed into matchless champions when the fate of the Cause of God is at stake.

It was in the pitch of night. The blasts of the enemy guns shattered the air, the flash from their muzzles punctuated the darkness, bullets and cannonballs whistled overhead. Ghulám-Riḍá instructed his troop of unlikely heroes to ride out of the fort, spread into a line, together raise the call of, 'God is most great!' and charge into the heart of the enemy.

Taking their rifles in hand, the fifteen Heroes leapt onto their horses and rode out to do battle. The shapes of their prancing horses were outlined against the flash of the enemy guns, the voices of young and old alike shouted 'God is most great!' and into the midst of their enemy they charged.

The battle raged for no less than eight hours. The rising sun gave witness to a fearless band of Heroes fighting with a courage and skill that amazed even the hardened veterans among the ranks of the enemy. The hearts of the townspeople watching the spectacle went out to the outnumbered Heroes. Many people, believing the gallant band was in the right, joined in to help them. The battle spread to the edge of the town, and from the rooftops the women began to cheer the Heroes on to victory. Their wild cheers, mixed with the war cries of Ghulám-Riḍá and his valiant men, added an unusual note to the roar of the battle.

At that point in the struggle the spirit of the enemy began to break. Demoralized and gripped with fear, they threw their weapons down, and scattered like leaves before the wind. The trenches were empty, the guns were silent, the camp was abandoned. Captain Ghulám-Riḍá had succeeded in his mission, but at a heavy price; many wounded and dead companions were carried back to Fort Khájih.

This crushing defeat drove home a truth the governor had, up to this point, been unwilling to accept: no force at his command could overcome these brave people. He decided to pursue another strategy: treachery! It came to him that through tricks and lies he could deceive the pure and noble hearts of the defenders within the fort. He ordered his troops to retreat for a few days, then he sent a message to Vaḥíd. He said that he had thought things over, and maybe he had been mistaken in his fear of Vaḥíd's new religion. He invited him to come out and explain its truth. He swore on the Qur'án that no harm would come to any of them. Setting his seal to that Holy Book, he sent it along with the message to Vaḥíd.

Vaḥíd received the Holy Qur'án with great reverence and kissed it devoutly. 'Our appointed hour has struck,' he remarked to his companions. 'Our acceptance of their invitation will surely make them feel the baseness of their treachery. Though I am well aware of their designs, I feel it my duty to accept their call and take the opportunity to attempt once again to unfold the truths of my beloved Faith.'

Bidding his companions farewell, Vaḥíd and five others, one of whom proved to be a traitor, set out for the camp of the governor. With great ceremony the governor and his officers received him in a tent especially prepared for the meeting. The power of his words were such that even the stone-hearted would not have failed to be moved. 'I am come to you,' he declared, 'armed with the testimony with which my Lord has entrusted me. Am I not a descendant of the Prophet of God? Wherefore should you have risen to slay me? For what reason have you pronounced my death-sentence, and refused to recognize the undoubted rights with which my lineage has invested me?'

Stunned by the majesty of his bearing and the eloquence of his words, they listened in rapt attention. For three days they lavishly entertained him and appeared to treat him with respect. But this was all an act. Secretly they were plotting the best way to kill him and his companions back at the fort. They were careful to not lay a finger on Vaḥíd, for they feared the wrath and vengeance of the Bábí forces if any harm were to come to him. They had to come up with a plan that was as foolproof as possible.

The governor decided to ask Vaḥíd to write a letter to his companions informing them that everything had been peacefully settled, and they could return to their homes. He knew it was a trick, but they put so much pressure on him that he finally did it. However, he secretly wrote a second letter warning his companions of the evil intentions of the governor. He entrusted both letters to one of the men who had accompanied him when he left the fort. He instructed him to destroy the first and deliver the second, and for them to issue forth in full attack upon the enemy.

This was the man who proved himself a traitor. Instead of following the wishes of Vaḥíd, he went straight to the governor and told him what Vaḥíd had instructed him to do. Promising him a rich reward, the governor induced him to deliver the first letter and to tell the defenders that the entire army had been converted to the Faith of the Báb, and that now they could go freely to their homes.

Betraying the trust of Vaḥíd, the man delivered the first letter and message to the fort. The companions were very displeased with these instructions, but felt they could not disobey what they believed to be the wishes of their leader, Vaḥíd. They gave up the fort and headed for town. They had not gone far before they realized they had fallen into a trap. Troops had been lying in wait, ready to ambush the unsuspecting Bábís. Suddenly they found themselves hemmed in on all sides. Fortunately, some were still carrying their arms and put up a fight. With cries of 'God is most great!' they battled their way into the city, and a few were cut down. Once inside they were separated and took cover in various parts of the city.

The governor had nothing to fear now that the Bábí forces were scattered. Disregarding his promise, he allowed the full force of his hatred for Vaḥíd to be set loose. He permitted that he be turned over to some men whose brothers and fathers had been killed in the battles with the Bábís. Thirst for revenge having erased every trace of mercy from their hearts, they leaped at this opportunity to kill Vaḥíd.

Snatching his turban from his head, they unwound the cloth, tied one end around his neck and the other to a horse. Applying a whip to its back, they galloped it through the streets dragging the blameless Vaḥíd behind it. His body at last coming to a stop, people heaped unspeakable indignities upon it. The foul women of the city, churned into murderous excitement by the gory scene, gathered around his precious frame. Witchlike, to the clash of cymbals and the beat of drums, they began a gruesome dance around the fallen Hero. It was a carnival of death!

Witnesses to the dreadful scene could not help but compare his end to the tragic death of the Imam Husayn centuries before. In the midst of his agony he had uttered the same words the Imam Husayn had spoken in similar circumstances centuries before: 'Thou knowest, O my Beloved, that I have abandoned the world for Thy sake, and have placed my trust in Thee alone. I am impatient to hasten to Thee, for the beauty of Thy countenance has been unveiled to my eyes. Thou dost witness the evil designs which my wicked persecutor has cherished against me. Nay, never will I submit to his wishes or pledge my allegiance to him.'

Thus ended the noble and distinguished life of Vaḥíd, Hero of God. Surely, so rare a man as he was worthy of a crown of martyrdom in circumstances so similar to those of the Imam Husayn.

The death of Vaḥíd was the signal to begin the murder of any who had accepted the Faith of the Báb. Men were seized, tortured and slaughtered. Women and children were captured and dealt brutalities no pen dare describe. Their homes were destroyed and their property taken. Most of the men were led in chains to Shiraz, and, for the most part, killed there. Some, the governor kept for his own purpose. They were thrown into his torture chambers where they were forced to undergo the most horrible forms of punishment. He hoped they might reveal the location of hidden riches he could seize for himself. Every imaginable kind of torture was devised to satisfy the thirst for revenge. They were branded, their fingernails were pulled out, spikes were hammered through their feet, and strings were run through their noses. In that pitiful condition they were led through the streets of Nayríz. In the end, each suffered a martyr's death.

The final act of this circus of horrors repeated the dramatic climax of the martyrdom of the Imam Husayn. The heads of the defeated were cut off, raised on spears and carried to Shiraz to be shown to the Prince as proof of what they thought was a victory over the Bábís.

But what they thought was a victory was, in truth, a shameful and damning defeat. For just as the story of the martyrdom of the Imam Husayn and his companions quickened the soul of man in a former age, so it was destined that the stories of the martyrdom of Vaḥíd and the rest of the immortals who adorn these pages are to quicken the soul of man in this age. And thus it shall forever be, that through such sacrifice, the forces of light are victorious over the forces of darkness.

CHAPTER EIGHT

ḤUJJAT
CAPTAIN OF THE HEROES
OF GOD AT ZANJÁN

Ḥujjat was the man who, after reading but one page of
the writings of the Báb, recognized that He was the Lord
of the Age, and bowed down in the mosque pledging to
Him his undying allegiance. Ḥujjat's father was one of
the leading priests of Zanján, and he was to follow in his
father's footsteps. From his early childhood, Ḥujjat had
shown a fiery zeal for the truth, and was always ready
to vigorously defend his point of view. His skill and
knowledge aroused the jealousy of some of the priests of
Zanján. Obeying his father's wishes, he took up residence
in a different city to avoid the venom of their hatred.

He had been away for three years when he received
news of his father's death, which made him decide to
return to Zanján. The great ovation with which the people
greeted him further aroused the hatred of the priests.

Ḥujjat's friends built a mosque in his honour adjoin-
ing that of his father. He used it to give lectures and lead
in prayer the multitudes who crowded within. He felt
that Islam had lost some of its purity. He spent seventeen

years urging his followers to live in strict accordance to the high standards of their Faith. His goal was to purify their hearts of whatever seemed contrary to the spirit of Islam. All the while his enemies hoped for an opportunity to bring him down.

As soon as he accepted the Cause of the Báb he began to teach its truth in the Mosque. Throngs of people gathered to listen, and were convinced to follow him in his new-found Faith. This gave his enemies a new approach in their efforts to rid themselves of him. 'His reputation for justice, for piety, wisdom, and learning', they whispered, 'has been such as to render it impossible for us to shake his position.'

'Now, however, that he has so openly championed the cause of the Siyyid-i-Báb, we can surely succeed in obtaining from the government the order for his arrest and banishment from our town.'

They sent their appeal to the Shah, hoping he would turn against Ḥujjat. This Shah had known Ḥujjat for some time and respected his knowledge and uprightness. Nevertheless, he wanted to get to the bottom of this controversy, so he ordered Ḥujjat and his opponents to come to the capital for a hearing. Ḥujjat answered every question to his complete satisfaction. The Shah rewarded him and bade him return to Zanján and continue his valuable services.

With increased vigour Ḥujjat continued to proclaim the fundamental teachings of the Faith of the Báb. A large portion of the citizens responded and accepted the Cause of God. The liberating principles he taught were a threat to the narrow and binding way the priests had used religion to oppress the people. It seemed to them that everything they had worked so long to build was crumbling away before their very eyes.

Then Ḥujjat received a momentous Tablet from the Báb. Among the instructions it contained was the command that he, Ḥujjat, was to lead the people in the Friday prayer. The head priest, who had performed this honour up to now, loudly protested on the grounds that this right had been conferred upon him by the Shah. Ḥujjat answered that the authority of the Lord of the Age was above that of even the Shah. 'I have', he added, 'been commanded by Him to assume that function publicly, and I cannot allow any person to trespass upon that right. If attacked, I will take steps to defend myself and to protect the lives of my companions.'

An unbridgeable gulf had opened between the followers of a newborn Faith and the leaders of an outworn and crumbling system.The priests joined together and brought their complaint this time to the head minister of the Shah, the Grand Vizier. Again the command of the king for Ḥujjat to come to the capital was issued.

Before Ḥujjat received the royal summons, he had heard that the Báb was being detained outside Tehran. He sent a message to his Lord begging to be allowed to come and rescue Him from His enemies. The Báb forbade this, answering that only the Almighty could achieve His deliverance. 'As to your meeting with Me,' He added, 'it soon will take place in the world beyond, the home of unfading glory.' This answer arrived the same day

91

Ḥujjat received the summons of the Shah.

A series of interviews followed in which Ḥujjat boldly, and with utmost skill, demonstrated the truth of his new-found Faith, and refuted the outrageous claims of his enemies. The Shah's continued favour for him was unshaken, and it was the only thing between him and death. The Grand Vizier disliked Ḥujjat and feared he was fast becoming a threat to the State. He made sure he was kept captive in Tehran where, isolated from his co-religionists, he hoped he could do less harm.

It happened that Bahá'u'lláh was in the city during this time and Ḥujjat was able to meet Him. He became completely devoted to Bahá'u'lláh. They received news of the dramatic events taking place at Fort Ṭabarsí. Ḥujjat longed to join that gallant band of men struggling for the freedom of their Faith. Bahá'u'lláh consoled him, and filled him with the sustaining power to enable him, in the very near future, to achieve equal deeds of heroism.

Concerned with the delay in Ḥujjat's return, his companions in Zanján sent enquiries to him as to what attitude they were to take towards the laws and principles of their new-found Faith. He sent them word that they were to faithfully follow, even as the Báb did himself, every teaching He had revealed, even if it appeared to be different from what they had done in the past. No sooner was this answer received than the companions enthusiastically set the old religious customs aside and put the new laws of God into effect. Even little children were encouraged to obey the commandments He had given. 'Our beloved Master', they were taught to say, 'Himself is the first to practise them.

Why should we who are His privileged disciples hesitate to make them the ruling principles of our lives."

Ḥujjat was still detained in the capital when alarming news reached him. The Shah who held him in such favour was dead, and his son, who held no such affection for Ḥujjat, had taken the throne. In addition, a new Grand Vizier had come to power, more ruthless than the one he replaced. Realizing the danger he was in, Ḥujjat fled from the capital in disguise and rejoined his companions in Zanján.

His arrival at the town was received with a tremendous demonstration of loyalty from the men, women and children who had come out to greet him. The governor was so infuriated by this that he ordered that the tongue of the one who announced Ḥujjat's coming be cut out. The governor's mind worked feverishly to find a way to destroy Ḥujjat.

The governor thought of a plan to enflame the situation even more. He ordered that a child be put under arrest for a trifling matter. Since the child was related to one of the companions, Ḥujjat sent a trusted friend to the governor's house to insist on the child's release. The governor resisted until the messenger threatened to force his way through the gate and use his sword, whereupon the child was released by the governor. The priests took this as a sign that Ḥujjat could get whatever he wanted from the governor. They went to him and protested violently, saying that this kind of submission by him to Ḥujjat would enable Ḥujjat to take over the government, leaving him, the governor, powerless. They demanded he arrest Ḥujjat to prevent the spread of his influence. Assured that this action would not endanger the peace, the governor agreed.

Two burly men, noted for their brutality, were recruited for the task. They were promised a rich reward to seize Ḥujjat and bring him in handcuffs to the Governor. Dressed in steel helmets and vests, and followed by the riff-raff of the city, they set out to complete the dastardly deed.

As they neared the home of Ḥujjat, their way was blocked by seven Bábís, led by a courageous man by the name of Salah. Facing the leader of the ruffians, Salah asked where they were headed. On receiving an insulting reply, he unsheathed his sword and let out a tremendous cry of 'O Lord of the Age!' His blade flashing in the sunlight, he sprang at the leader, wounding him on the forehead despite his heavy armour. Frightened by this display of fearlessness, the whole gang turned tail and beat a path in the opposite direction.

The tension between the Bábís on one side and the priests and governor on the other had reached breaking point. Later that day some of the riff-raff who had run in terror before the courage of Salah came upon one unarmed Bábí. They pounced upon him and wounded him with an axe. They carried him to the home of the governor where he and his henchmen took turns in stabbing him until he died a martyr's death. Unmindful of his suffering, he was heard to say, 'I thank Thee, O my God, for having vouchsafed me the crown of martyrdom.'

So began the upheaval of Zanján, a tale whose agony was to be unsurpassed even in the bloodthirsty annals of the century. The date was 16 May 1850. The name of this

Bábí was Shaykh Muḥammad-i-Túb-Chí, and his was the first blood shed in the town of Zanján. It was forty-five days before the martyrdom of Vaḥíd and fifty-five days before the martyrdom of the Báb.

Unsatisfied with this dirty deed, the enemy wanted to put to death every follower of a religion they were convinced would destroy everything in which they believed. They sent a crier throughout the city announcing that anyone on the side of Ḥujjat and the Báb would lose their lives and their property, and that their wives and children would be put to shame.

This warning immediately divided the people into two camps and tested the faith of those who were unsure of their belief in the Cause of the Báb. A great tumult was raised from the people. Fathers were separated from sons, brothers from brothers, the faithful from the faint-hearted, the sheep from the goats. On one side were heard the cries of distress and despair of people watching their loved ones breaking with them to join the Cause of the Lord of the Age. On the other, the jubilant shouts of happy excitement of those who tore themselves from every tie, and enrolled in the cause of Ḥujjat. A verse in the Qur'án had said, 'Do men think when they say "We believe" they shall be let alone and not be put to proof?' This fateful hour had now struck.

Ḥujjat climbed into the pulpit and spoke: 'The Hand of Omnipotence has, in this day, separated truth from falsehood and divided the light of guidance from the darkness of error. I am unwilling that because of me you should suffer injury.'

As the Bábís prepared to defend themselves, Ḥujjat called on his followers to never attack, but to defend themselves to the end. 'Brothers,' he called, 'do not be ashamed of me. Do not think that because you are the companions of the Lord of the Age you must conquer the world by the sword. No, I take God as my witness. They will kill you, they will burn you, they will send your heads from town to town. The only victory in store for you is to sacrifice yourselves – you, your wives and your possessions. God has decreed that in every age the blood of the believers is to be the oil of the lamp of religion . . . I say unto you, whosoever has not the strength to bear such torment, let him go over to the other side, for we will have to endure martyrdom.'

As this was happening, the enemies began to organize every available resource to destroy Ḥujjat and his people. The enemy camp stirred with activity. More than three thousand men were recruited to join in the struggle against the Bábís. Salah, alarmed at these preparations, went to Ḥujjat and urged him to make plans to protect themselves. Nearby was a well-constructed group of houses. Ḥujjat made arrangements to trade some of the Bábí homes for them. Then he ordered his wife and children and all the Bábí families – women, youth and children included – to take up residence within. They carried their food, supplies and arms with them. The houses hummed with activity as the Bábís put everything in good order.

Supporters of the governor made a few feeble attempts to dislodge the Bábís, but with no results. Ḥujjat had to hold back the men who were so eager to punish the enemy. 'We are commanded', he frequently told them, 'not to wage holy war against the unbelievers, whatever be their attitude towards us.'

This continued until a royal order issued by the Grand Vizier reached the general of two imperial regiments in the area. The order commanded him to march to Zanján and crush the Bábís. It promised that his success would win the royal favour of the Shah. Puffed up with pride, the general arrived upon the scene and took command of the combined forces arrayed against Ḥujjat and his companions. He ordered the siege of the Bábí houses to begin.

It was the glorious story of Fort Ṭabarsí all over again. Day after day the enemy forces attacked and bombarded the Bábí houses; time after time the Heroes of God would charge out before their adversaries, and answering their curses with the cry 'O Lord of the Age!' administer to them a punishing defeat. For three days and three nights the Heroes delivered such blows to the enemy that their will to fight left them. The crestfallen general was in command of a mere thirty crippled and beaten soldiers. The remainder had either fallen before the swords of the Bábís, or deserted the fight. Totally humiliated, the general was stripped of his rank, scolded by the Shah, and sent away in shame.

During times of relative quiet Ḥujjat took measures to strengthen their defences. He directed his companions to build twenty-eight barricades in front of the houses; to each he assigned thirty-eight men, nineteen to be stationed at the barricades and nineteen who were to act as look-outs. In addition, he gave orders that tunnels be dug under the houses in which the women and children could take shelter during attack. Their refuge had been transformed into a fortress.

Whereas fresh reinforcements continued to arrive from Tehran, increasing the strength of the attackers, the food and supplies of the Bábís slowly dwindled to practically nothing. Hunger and weakness began to take their toll, and little by little, battle by battle, they were being whittled down.

About this time the governor thought up a scheme to tempt the gallant defenders. Between battles he sent a messenger to within earshot of the Bábís. The messenger would shout to them that if any one of them would renounce his faith in the Báb, he would be forgiven, could go freely on his way and would be richly rewarded by the Shah. What was their answer? Shouting together, with one mighty voice they proclaimed they would never deny their Faith.

Zaynab, the Maid of God

Among the gallant defenders was a beautiful local girl named Zaynab, from one of the nearby villages. Together with the women and children she watched the bravery and hardship of the men defending their posts. An uncontrollable urge began to grow in her breast. She wished that she could, somehow, stand sword in hand and do battle at their sides. This passion took such complete control of her that she cut her hair, disguised herself as a man, took up sword and shield and boldly took her place at the barricades.

With throbbing heart she waited for her first taste of battle. At last the moment came. As the enemy moved forward in full attack, she held her sword high, and in a piercing voice raised the cry 'O Lord of the Age!' Over the top she went, meeting the charging soldiers head on, swinging her sword to and fro with mighty sweeps, cutting down any who dared to face her. Her companions and enemy alike marvelled at her courage and might. The enemy fell back before her awesome power.

Eagle-eyed, Ḥujjat was watching the battle from a look-out tower behind the barricades. He recognized Zaynab in spite of her disguise. Watching her pursuing the retreating enemy, he sent command that she be called back and brought before him. Ḥujjat took her aside, and in the most gentle way, questioned her as to why she, a young girl, was out fighting beside the men. Tears streaming from her eyes, she explained, 'My heart ached with pity and sorrow when I beheld the toil and sufferings of my fellow disciples. I advanced by an inner urge I could not resist.' She begged that Ḥujjat allow her to continue to bear arms for her Lord.

He must have fought to hold back his own tears, as he gazed upon this tender young girl, in the sweet bloom of youth, standing life in hand in service to her Lord. After giving her the name Rustam-'Alí after two legendary heroes of old, he told her, 'This is the Day of Resurrection, the day when "all secrets shall be searched out". Not by their outward appearance, but by the character of their beliefs and the manner of their lives, does God judge His creatures, be they men or women. Though a maiden of tender age and immature experience, you have displayed such vitality and resource as few men could hope to surpass.' He granted her request. From that day forward Zaynab was unmatched in zeal, daring and courage. Her sword and shield never left her side, and when she slept her trusty blade served as her pillow and her shield as her cover; ever ready was she to answer the call of duty.

Every Bábí was instructed by Ḥujjat to remain fixed at his post along the barricades; only the Maid of God, Zaynab, was allowed to move freely along the lines during battle. Back and forth she would storm, encouraging her companions on to greater effort. At whatever point the enemy would direct their charge, she would rush into the gap and beat them back.

In time her secret became known to the enemy, and, in spite of their knowledge that she was just a young girl, the soldiers would tremble when she came into the field of battle, for so many of them had fallen before her sure sword. The mere shrill sound of her voice would take the fight completely out of them. They believed she was the curse that an angry God had sent upon them.

One fateful day Zaynab knew her time on earth had come to an end. The enemy had mounted a strong attack, and it appeared the Bábí line would be over-run. Realizing she was needed as never before, she ran to her Captain, Ḥujjat, and threw herself at his feet, begging that he permit her to rush to their aid. Tearfully she implored him, 'My life, I feel, is nearing its end. I may myself fall beneath the sword of the assailant. Forgive me, I entreat you, my trespasses, and intercede for me with my Master, for whose sake I yearn to lay down my life.'

Ḥujjat was too choked with emotion to reply; but she saw the answer she desired in the eyes of her Captain. Her tears swept from her eyes, joy filled her heart. Up and away she ran, on to the field of battle she went. Surveying the scene, she darted to the point where the enemy was about to break through. Into the centre she rushed, calling on the Lord of the Age seven times. Back fell the enemy.

'Why befoul by your deeds the fair name of Islam?' she shouted. With each forward step she took, her sword cut further into the ranks of the foe. 'Why flee abjectly-from before our face, if you be speakers of truth?' she cried. Gripped by fear, the soldiers retreated to their own barricades. Onward charged the Maid of God, capturing three of the barricades of the enemy. At this moment of her supreme effort, her glorious end came. A troop of riflemen sent a shower of bullets that struck her and she fell dead upon the ground. The Maid of God, Zaynab, Rustam-'Alí, passed from this world to the kingdom of wonders beyond.

And now, dear reader, her story has been told. Wonderstruck, the shining spirit that animated her devotion thrills our very souls. Brimming over, our love for her cannot be contained. Never-fading, her image shimmers in our mind's eye. For we have seen the glory of the Lord manifest in the flaming, divine passion of Zaynab, the Maid of God, forever enshrined among that hallowed band of the Heroes of the New Age.

****

One night during a lull between battles, the camp of the enemy was filled with the sounds of cursing, drunken laughter, gambling, and the giggling of loose women. Ḥujjat instructed the defenders of the barricades to repeat nineteen times the invocations commanded by the Báb. The Bábí men raised their united voices in praise of God. The repeated strains of 'God the Most Great! God the Most Pure! God the Most Beauteous! God the Most Glorious!' began to pierce the night air. Gathering momentum, the sound amplified and roared into the camp of the frolicking enemy. Thinking the Bábís were upon them, the officers dropped their wine glasses and ran for the woods; soldiers dove for cover, upsetting their gambling tables, and others bolted from their tents half-dressed and barefooted. Others dropped dead on the spot from sheer fright. Some believed it was the sign of the Day of Judgement; others believed it to be the prelude to an offensive by the Bábís more terrible than anything they had yet experienced. What a stark contrast between the devout Heroes of God and a low-minded enemy!

As the siege wore on, Ḥujjat decided to write to the Shah assuring him of his loyalty and requesting his protection. He explained that this controversy was primarily with the priests of the city who had misrepresented the situation. No sooner had the messenger set out to deliver the appeal to the Shah, than he was seized and taken before the governor. Infuriated by the content of the message, he had the messenger put to death. He destroyed the letters, wrote new ones filled with insults, forged the signature of Ḥujjat and sent them to the Shah. Enraged at the content of the forged letters, the King commanded that not one Bábí be left alive. Armies were organized; guns and ammunition were gathered; a general was appointed to direct the destruction of the Bábís at Zanján.

It was at about this time that the news of the martyrdom of the Báb reached Zanján. (This story will be told in the next chapter.) The enemy thought that this news would break the spirit of the Bábís. The soldiers taunted and ridiculed the Heroes. Shouting scornfully, they asked why they should be willing to sacrifice themselves now that their Master was gone; why not surrender, give up their Faith and go free. These efforts failed to convince even one of the companions to desert their Cause.

The general arrived from Tehran with seventeen regiments of footsoldiers, horsemen and fourteen big guns. In addition, five regiments were recruited from the surrounding area. The general decided to deliver an attack so destructive that none could survive. The very night of his arrival, he ordered that the trumpets be sounded and the attack begin. The booming of the cannons was so loud it could be heard for miles around.

Day after day went by, but the victory for which the general so hoped escaped his grasp. His best officers had been killed and the others who remained alive were completely demoralized and unwilling to obey his orders. His efforts to prevent additional supporters and supplies from getting through to the Bábís were completely frustrated. The news of his failure aroused the anger of the Grand Vizier, who sent him a letter informing him that unless he destroyed the Bábís immediately, he, the Grand

103

Vizier, would come personally to Zanján, strip him of his rank and massacre everyone in the town, regardless of their position or beliefs.

In a frenzy of desperation, the general called his remaining officers, the city officials, village chiefs and priests to a special meeting. He showed them the letter from the Grand Vizier and said that if they failed to arise and destroy the Bábís, it would mean their own destruction.

The next day every able-bodied man was assembled. To the beat of drums and the sound of trumpets a vast multitude marched on the Bábís. Calmly watching the approaching host, Ḥujjat gave the command to open the gates. Shouting together the cry 'O Lord of the Age!' out poured the companions, women and youths included.

This was the most ruthless and vicious battle to date. The enemy savagely tore at the Bábí defence. The best of Ḥujjat's men fell victim to the rabid enemy. Many a son was butchered before his mother's eyes, while sisters watched in horror as the heads of their loved ones were raised on spears. Resisting the fury of the enemy, the Bábís held their ground. The Bábí women struggled side by side with the men, encouraging them and aiding them in any way they could. When the two home-made guns they had were fired so often that they began to fall apart, the women cut their hair and wound the thick coils around the guns to hold them together. When a man fell wounded, a woman in men's clothing would pick up his weapon and stand fast in his place. For hours the battle raged. The warriors of God would not be defeated. Fighting a losing battle, the enemy began to falter. In confusion,

104

many deserted the field and the rest were trapped at the mercy of the Bábís. The victory achieved that day was due in large part to the encouraging shouts of the women, their heroism and self- sacrifice. But it was costly. No less than three hundred Bábí heroes fell in that battle.

The rigour and endurance demanded of the companions was beyond description. The high spirits and limitless enthusiasm that glowed so constant in the hearts of those valiant souls is impossible to portray. The effort made by the women was no less spectacular than that of the men. They worked with the men to keep everything in good order. They sewed the garments, baked the bread, nursed the sick and wounded, repaired the barricades, cleared the cannon shot and rubble left by the enemy, joined the fight when needed, and, last but not least, instilled into the men the moral courage to meet every ordeal. So solid was their spirit of unity that the enemy believed their number to be no less than ten thousand!

Among the brave company of Bábís were about one hundred unmarried youth. For each young man Ḥujjat chose a bride; these he joined in holy wedlock. He sold his last possessions to pay for a great wedding festival for the newlyweds. For a period of three months the gaiety continued. Only when the alarm was sounded would each of the young Heroes pause to leave the side of his bride. Tenderly she would embrace her husband and ask that he stay just a while longer, for this could be their last moment together. 'I can spare no time,' he would say. 'I must hasten to obtain the crown of glory. We shall surely meet again on the shores of the great Beyond, the home of blissful and eternal reunion.' Then he would jump to his feet, and with a last kiss instantly rush out to throw back the invaders. Eventually, one by one, each of the young bridegrooms gave his life for his Faith and won his eternal crown of glory.

Among the young husbands were five brothers who had joined with their father on the side of Ḥujjat. Ḥujjat had joined them in marriage with Bábí maidens during the great wedding festival. The ceremonies were hardly ended when cries of alarm called them to their posts. Leaving the sides of their loved ones, they took up their weapons, rushed to the barricades and threw back the enemy. In the course of that fierce battle all five of them fell bravely at the hand of the foe. The oldest, a youth noted for his steel-like nerve, was captured alive and taken to the enemy general. Venting his fury upon the noble youth, he ordered that he be pinned to the ground and a fire be started on his chest to burn the love of Ḥujjat out of him. 'Wretched man,' replied the young man, without even blinking an eye, 'no flame that the hands of your men are able to kindle could destroy the love that glows in my heart.' The name of his beloved Báb was on his lips until the flames had consumed his last breath.

As the battles wore on the inevitable truth became clear to the general: he would never honourably defeat the Bábís. Faced on one side with the unyielding resistance of Ḥujjat, and on the other the unending complaints of the Grand Vizier, he decided to resort to treachery. First he ordered an end to the attack, and then he started a rumour that the Shah wished to settle peacefully with Ḥujjat. After waiting for this lie to take hold, he sent a letter to Ḥujjat expressing his wish to settle everything peacefully. He sent along with the letter a copy of the Holy Qur'án as a token of his sincerity, hoping this would conceal his deceit.

Ḥujjat reverently received the Qur'án and then read the letter. Turning to his companions, he said that this was the same deceit as had been used at Ṭabarsí and Nayríz. Nevertheless, in respect for the holy Qur'án he would send a delegation to the camp of the general to expose his treachery. The delegation he chose was made up of nine boys, none of whom was more than ten years old, and some elderly men, none of whom were less than eighty years of age.

When they arrived at the headquarters of the general, he treated them with contempt. The most distinguished of the old men attempted to explain that they were completely loyal to the Shah, and it was only because the government had failed to protect them from persecution that they had taken up arms in self-defence. He reminded the general of the promise he had made to them, and held up the Qur'án he had sent to Ḥujjat.

This threw the general into a rage. His treachery exposed, he ordered that the old man's beard be torn out by the roots and the rest of them be thrown into a dungeon. With this, the children scurried through the arms of their captors and headed for the protection of their barricades. Some were overtaken, but at least one escaped and lived to tell the tale. Here is that story in his own words: 'As I was fleeing, the man who was pursuing me laid hold of the hem of my garment. I tore myself away from him and managed to reach the gate that led to the approaches of the fort, in a state of utter exhaustion. How great was my surprise when I saw one of the companions . . . being savagely mutilated by the enemy. I was horrified as I gazed upon that scene . . . I was soon informed that the victim had been betrayed by his brother, who, on the pretext of desiring to speak with him, had handed him over to his persecutors.

'I straightway went to Ḥujjat, who lovingly received me and, wiping the dust from my face, and clothing me with new garments, invited me to be seated by his side and bade me tell him the fate of his companions. I described to him all that I had seen.'

'It is the tumult of the Day of Resurrection,' Ḥujjat patiently explained to the child. It was the day foretold in the Holy Books, the day when a man would turn away from brother, mother, father, wife and child; the day when, as described in the Qur'án as well as the Bible, a mother would forsake her suckling babe, and every woman would cast her burden; when men would act drunkenly without having drank, and, not content with abandonment, would seek to shed the blood of their kinsmen.

Ḥujjat then assembled the entire Bábí host. He arose and spoke to them these words: 'I am well pleased with your unflinching endeavours, my beloved companions. Our enemies are bent upon our destruction. They harbour no other desire. Their intention was to trick you into coming out of the fort, and then to slaughter you mercilessly after their hearts' desire. Finding that their treachery has been exposed, they have, in the fury of their rage, ill-treated and imprisoned the oldest and the youngest among you. It is clear that not until they capture this fort and scatter you, will they lay down their arms or cease to persecute you. Your continued presence in this fort will eventually cause you to be taken captive by the enemy, who will of a certainty dishonour your wives and slay your children. Better is it, therefore, for you to make your escape in the middle of the night and to take your wives and children with you. Let each one seek a place of safety until such time as this tyranny shall be overpast. I shall remain alone to face the enemy. It were better that my death should allay their thirst for revenge than that you should all perish.'

Tears streamed from the eyes of his listeners while they declared their resolve to remain by his side regardless of the consequences. 'We can never consent to leave you to the mercy of a murderous enemy!' they exclaimed. 'Our lives are not more precious than your life . . . Whatever calamity may yet befall you, is what we shall welcome for ourselves.'

A few, unable to withstand the terror before them, followed the advice of Ḥujjat and found safety outside of the fort.

The general now reorganized and reinforced his troops. More men and cannons were brought in. He ordered that eight regiments attack every morning from dawn until noon, and then a fresh eight regiments would take their place and continue the attack until dark. For one month they blasted away at the Bábís, occasionally attacking at night. The fierceness of the relentless attack and the strength of the enemy numbers began to wear the defenders thin. Outside supplies were completely cut off, and misery and hunger also took their toll. At this desperate point, to the dismay of the Bábís, a special regiment arrived, equipped with large cannons. A withering stream of fire was directed at the Bábí stronghold. During the bombardment the companions fought with such valour that even their bitter enemy had to confess admiration.

As the enemy attack gained in strength, tragedy struck: Ḥujjat was offering his prayers when a bullet wounded him in the arm. His wife rushed to his side, only to find him completely calm, continuing his prayer. Blood pouring from the wound, he called to his Lord: 'Pardon this people, O God, for they know not what they do. Have mercy upon them, for they who have led them astray are alone responsible for the misdeeds the hands of this people have wrought.' Calming the fear of his wife and family at the sight of his blood-soaked clothes, Ḥujjat told them to rejoice and be content with the will and decree of God. This wound would prove fatal, but not for a while yet.

As word that Ḥujjat was wounded spread among the defenders, anguished cries of 'My Captain! My Captain!' must have swelled in their breasts as the entire company rushed to his side. Observing the Bábí posts temporarily unmanned, the enemy seized upon this priceless opportunity to attack without resistance. Over the rubble they charged, bursting through the gates and capturing no fewer than one hundred women and children. Their outer defences destroyed, the companions fell back and took new positions around the house of Ḥujjat, where the remaining women and children huddled for protection.

Regrouping, they divided into five companies made

up of nineteen squads composed of nineteen men to each squad. This added up to a total of 1,805 able-bodied men. Each company sent one squad, forming a troop of ninety-five men, to be on the alert to repel any move by the enemy. At the first sign of attack, the troop standing guard would shout at the top of their voices 'O Lord of the Age!' This alone would be enough to paralyse the will and crush the spirit of the enemy. The cornered Heroes met every attempt to dislodge them with deadly force. The enemy's casualties were such that officers began deserting their posts, artillery captains left their guns, and the demoralized soldiers refused to fight.

The general could not keep from his mind the threat of the Grand Vizier: the survival of the Bábís would mean the loss of his own life as well as those of the citizens of Zanján. 'I am weary,' he confessed, 'of the grim resistance of this people. They are moved by a spirit that no amount of encouragement from our sovereign can hope to call forth from our men . . . No power I can command is able to arouse my men from the slough of despair into which they have fallen. Whether they triumph or fail, these soldiers believe themselves doomed to eternal damnation.'

The general racked his brain to think of an approach that would not depend on the bravery of his men. He hit upon the idea to dig a tunnel that would reach under the houses that remained standing, and then put explosives underneath them to blow them up. He put his soldiers to work digging these tunnels. After digging for a whole month, they filled the tunnels with explosives and blew some of the houses to bits. Most of the buildings that surrounded the home of Ḥujjat were destroyed in the explosion, and the houses that remained standing were easy targets. Now the general ordered that the big guns be rolled into position and fired point-blank into them.

Inside his house, Ḥujjat was comforting his wife, who was holding their baby son in her arms. Suddenly a cannon-ball came crashing through the walls, killing her and injuring the infant, who would die from its injuries later.

Though crushed with grief, Ḥujjat would never yield to sorrow. He cried aloud: 'The day whereon I found Thy beloved One, O my God, and recognized in Him the Manifestation of Thy eternal Spirit, I foresaw the woes I should suffer for Thee. Great as have been until now my sorrows, they can never compare with the agonies that I would willingly suffer in Thy name. How can this miserable life of mine, the loss of my wife and of my child, and the sacrifice of the band of my kindred and companions, compare with the blessings which the recognition of Thy Manifestation has bestowed on me! Would that a myriad lives were mine, would that I possessed the riches of the whole earth and its glory, that I might resign them all freely and joyously in Thy path.'

The companions were filled with the desire to avenge the loss sustained by their leader, but he commanded them to restrain themselves and be steadfast to the end, resigning themselves to the will of God as the enemy continued to rain down destruction upon their houses.

Ḥujjat's wound had been draining his life away for nineteen days. That life was now to reach its end. Wounded unto death, he must have yearned to pass into that divine eternal world where his Beloved awaited him. He lay prostrate on the ground, calling the name of the Báb, when he suddenly passed away.

The death of their intrepid leader shocked and grieved the companions. His loss was the greatest blow they could suffer. They buried his body in the ruins, hoping the enemy would never find it. In spite of the loss of their Captain, the companions continued to resist the attacks of the enemy with indomitable courage. But the battles, bombardments and butcheries, the explosions, treacheries and murders had gradually reduced them to two hundred able-bodied men. About five hundred women and the wounded men had taken shelter in Ḥujjat's house.

The news of the death of Ḥujjat renewed the hopes of the enemy. Gathering together every resource at their disposal, they launched a general attack. To the sounds of shouting, trumpets and drums, the wild mass of people moved forward, determined to destroy the companions once and for all. Their leader gone, their defences destroyed, and hopelessly outnumbered, the companions nevertheless took courage. Once again they raised the call 'O Lord of the Age!' and confronted their foe. Resisting with the last ounce of their strength, they fought as bravely as they ever had; but the ferocious multitude was overwhelming. One by one they were either killed or captured.

With the capture of the last Bábí, the pent-up vengeance of the enemy was set loose. A reign of terror began. First they robbed all the valuables they could find in the wrecked houses. Next, the priests excited the populace into a lawless mob, encouraging the torture of the men and the dishonouring of the women. Then the women were rounded up and robbed by a greedy priest and sent, despoiled, to their relatives. The wounded were set out in the cold without medical attention until they perished. The male captives were sentenced to die. Seventy-six companions were forced to march to the beat of drums to the camp of the army. The soldiers competed with each other as to who could devise the most gruesome torture. With lances and spears they mutilated them; with whips they lashed them; with bars they beat them; with cannons they blew them to kingdom come. The horror was disgusting beyond words.

One of the companions, in the sufferings of death, pealed out the cry 'God is most great!' Part of the enemy army included a regiment from Iraq. Upon hearing this call, they refused to take any further part in the bloodshed and horror. They no longer believed the Bábís were a godless people.

Despite the horrible tortures the companions were made to suffer, not a word of anger passed from their lips; not a whisper of pain escaped their mouths; not a shadow of discontent could be seen in their faces. It was as if they had already entered that world of unending delight.

Their loathsome pleasures unsatisfied, the army now searched for the body of Ḥujjat. The ghoulish governor wanted his corpse. His tortures had failed to get a single companion to reveal the spot where his remains were hidden. He called for Ḥujjat's seven-year-old son to be brought to him.

Talking to the child sweetly, he said that it was not

himself who had caused the death of his parents, rather, the priests were the guilty ones. He told the child that if he would just show him where his papa was buried they could have a nice funeral for him. The innocent child believed this lie, and showed him where his father was buried. Fiendishly, the governor then ordered the body of Ḥujjat be dug up and dragged through the streets of Zanján to the sound of drums and trumpets. He then ordered that it be left out in the public square for the people to heap more injuries upon it. After three days of unspeakable desecration the remains were taken away.

The upheaval of Zanján is ended. But the name Ḥujjat shall never be forgotten. Ḥujjat means 'the Proof' in English. He was a man who had everything – fame, family, fortune and friends, all the things people think will bring them happiness in this life. But he was inspired by a higher love, a higher loyalty, the sublime vision of the Kingdom of God and an overpowering love for the Manifestation of God! And for this reason he sacrificed everything the world holds dear. It was the Báb Who conferred upon him the name Ḥujjat. Could it be that the story of his life, entailing as it does such clear choices, be sufficient proof of the superior worth of the choice he made?

Today Zanján sits quietly in a long valley between two ranges of mountains. Because its soil is stained with the blood of uncounted martyrs, the Báb gave it a new name, 'the Exalted Spot', and by this name the world shall ever know it.

CHAPTER NINE

THE MÁRTYRDOM
OF THE BÁB

The successive waves of violence that battered the infant Cause of God had taken their toll. Quddús, Mullá Ḥusayn, Vaḥíd and more than half the Letters of the Living had fallen at the hands of the enemies of God. Countless others shed their blood to nourish the Tree of Life. The Báb had been kept isolated for nearly three years. Yet, in spite of it all, the Cause of God continued to move across the land. The horrible tortures, the mass deaths, betrayals and imprisonments only fanned the flames of faith into a more brilliant light.

The priests and officials did not understand the real effect of their persecution of the Bábís. Interference in matters of belief and conscience only causes the belief of most of those persecuted to become more firm, and, in addition, it draws public attention to the new way of thinking that brought on the persecution in the first place. As a result, the interest of people is aroused, and they are moved to examine the matter very carefully. Ever-growing numbers of people become sympathetic to the new way of thinking, support its followers, and eventually embrace its cause. This is the reason why persecution in matters of belief is a blessing in disguise.

The Grand Vizier understood this to some degree, nevertheless he mistakenly believed that the Bábí movement was too great a threat to the Kingdom to be allowed to continue. One of his ministers protested against the thought of killing the Báb, pointing out to the Vizier the fact that the Báb was a descendant of the Prophet Muhammad. The Grand Vizier reminded him that even the Imam Husayn of old, who was the Grandson of the Prophet Muhammad Himself, was put to death because he was a threat to the State. He said the only way to put an end to the new religion would be to destroy the life of its founder, the Báb Himself.

The Báb was aware that His days on earth were nearing their end. Throughout His ministry He had made references to Bahá'u'lláh, indicating that He was the One for whom He was preparing the way. His martyrdom approaching, He composed a Tablet and sent it to Bahá'u'lláh. Consisting of three hundred and sixty different ways to say 'Bahá', it was a magnificent glorification of His Holy Name. The letters, written on a sheet of clear blue paper, were composed in the form of a five-pointed star, symbolizing the physical temple of Bahá'u'lláh. The penmanship was so fine that the letters appeared from a distance as a wash of ink upon the blue.

The Grand Vizier feared that if he were to execute the Báb in the capital city of Tehran, a revolution could break out. He decided to send Him to Tabriz, a city in a far corner of the kingdom. He issued the order that the Báb be taken directly to the house of a priest in that city.

For about three days he tried to get the prince of the region to carry out the order of execution, but with no success. The prince refused to do it, saying he would not act in the same manner as the persecutors of the Imam Husayn, long ago. Frustrated with this refusal, the Grand Vizier asked his own brother to do the awful deed, and he agreed to do it. He ordered guards to take the Báb from the house of the priest to the army barracks near the centre of the city, and that He be executed the next day, along with any of his followers who refused to deny their Faith.

As the guards began to march the Báb through the city, a strange force began to take hold of the people. Crowds began to gather and follow him on his way. The feeling of the coming of the Day of Doom began to spread among the people. By the time He arrived at the barracks masses of them were surging on all sides. Suddenly, out of the crowd a high-born youth by the name of Muḥammad-'Alí broke through and cast himself at the feet of the Báb. Clutching the hem of His robe he begged, 'Send me not from Thee, O Master. Wherever Thou goest, suffer me to follow Thee.'

Gazing at the youth kneeling before Him, the Báb answered, 'Muḥammad-'Alí, arise, and rest assured that you will be with Me. Tomorrow you shall witness what God has decreed.' He gave the young man the title 'Anís', meaning 'Companion'.

Two other young men also rushed forward and pledged to the Báb their undying loyalty. And the Báb accepted them. These two along with Anís were cast into a cell with the Báb. It is beyond human ability to imagine the meeting of these souls with the Messenger of God in these terrible conditions; how spiritual sublimity emerged out of a darksome death cell. But this much we know: one of the young men who entered the cell was named Siyyid Ḥusayn. The Báb desired that he be left alive to tell the story of what had happened. He commanded him not to confess his new-found Faith so that he be left alive to tell the tale of those final moments. Siyyid Ḥusayn obeyed the Báb and survived. Here is the story he told of what happened in the cell.

'That night the face of the Báb was aglow with joy, a joy such as had never shone from His countenance. Indifferent to the storm that raged about Him, He conversed with us with gaiety and cheerfulness. The sorrows that had weighed so heavily upon Him seemed to have completely vanished. Their weight appeared to have dissolved in the consciousness of approaching victory.'

The Báb told them He would prefer to be slain by the hand of one of them than by the enemy. Two of the young men were horrified at such a thought, but not Anís. Leaping to his feet, he announced his desire to obey whatever the Báb might desire. 'This same youth who has arisen to comply with My wish', declared the Báb, 'will, together with me, suffer martyrdom. Him will I choose to share with Me its crown.'

Next morning the guards arrived at the cell where the Báb was being held. They explained to Him that their orders were that He be taken to the leading priests of the city to obtain their authorization for His execution. At this moment the Báb was in the midst of a conversation with Siyyid Ḥusayn. The head guard pulled the disciple away, saying it was time for them to go to see the priests. Suddenly the Báb's power surged forth. He declared, 'Not until I have said to him all those things that I wish to say can any earthly power silence Me. Though all the world be armed against Me, yet shall they be powerless to deter Me from fulfilling, to the last word, My intention.' Amazed at this reply, the guard continued to carry out his order. Soon he would learn the truth of these words.

Iron collars were placed around the necks of the Báb and Anís, leashes were tied to the collars and guards led them through the city. The march to the homes of the priests had begun. Since the day before, the town had been growing wild with excitement. Crowds gathered to follow Him along His way. With each step the emotions of the rabble of the city, whipped into hatred by the priests, rose to a higher pitch. Following along, they shouted insults, and pelted the prisoners with stones. When they came to the door of each one of the priests' houses not a single one would come out to see the Báb face to face. Hurriedly, they signed the execution order and passed it through the doorway.

The shameful business finished, that same morning a regiment of seven hundred and fifty riflemen had been brought to the barracks and lined up to perform the execution. From the time the guards had entered the cell of the Báb that morning to take Him to the priests the captain of the regiment had been standing by watching the Báb and all that had happened.

The noble and dignified behaviour of the Báb had a deep effect on the captain. He wondered at the possibility that He really was God's Messenger, and he feared the wrath of God if he were to participate in His death. To put his mind at ease, he went to the Báb and said: 'I profess the Christian Faith and entertain no ill will against you. If your Cause be the Cause of Truth, enable me to free myself from the obligation to shed your blood.'

'Follow your instructions,' replied the Báb, 'and if your intention is sincere, the Almighty is surely able to relieve you from your perplexity.'"

Satisfied with this answer, the captain began to prepare for the execution. He ordered that a spike be hammered into the wall outside the cell where the Báb had been confined, and two ropes be tied to it. A rope was tied under each of the arms of the Báb and Anís in such a way that they were left suspended above the ground. Anís begged the captain to let his own body shield that of the Báb, and came to rest with his head against the Báb's breast.

All was ready. The captain ordered his men to form a firing squad composed of three rows of two hundred and fifty riflemen each. Looking up, he gazed along the rooftops at the teeming crowds gathered to see the spectacle. What thoughts must have raced through his head as he prepared to give the order to fire; oh! how the words of assurance to him from the Báb must have filled his thoughts. Trusting in those words, he gave the order to fire.

The riflemen raised their guns, took aim, and at his command, fired. A deafening boom from the seven hundred and fifty rifles shattered the silence; a huge cloud of smoke filled the air, blinding everyone. As the smoke cleared an amazing scene was unveiled to their eyes. The ropes were dangling in shreds; Anís was standing unharmed on the ground, and the Báb had disappeared from sight!

The head guard ordered an immediate search for the Báb. Looking everywhere, they finally found Him where they least expected – back in His cell, sitting quietly, without a scratch, completing His conversation with Siyyid Ḥusayn. The head guard could hardly believe his eyes; like a distant echo haunting his mind, he must have remembered those words spoken to him earlier by the Báb: 'Not until I have said to him all those things that I wish to say can any earthly power silence Me.'

In dumb silence, he stared at the Báb. The Báb calmly looked at him and said, 'I have finished My conversation with Siyyid Ḥusayn. Now you may proceed to fulfil your intention.' Too shaken by this display of the power of the Báb, he could not resume the task. He turned and walked away, resigning his post on the spot.

The captain of the regiment was stunned as well by the turn of events. In wonder he remembered the assurance made to him by the Báb after he had expressed his misgivings to Him. He swore he would have no further part in this affair, even if it cost him his life, and then he ordered his men to pack up their guns and march immediately from that place.

A hard-hearted colonel of the bodyguard volunteered to carry out the order of execution, and his regiment was brought in. Again the Báb and Anís were suspended in the same place and in the same manner. Again the regiment prepared to carry out the execution. Just before the command was given to fire, the Báb delivered His last words to the gazing multitudes: 'Had you believed in me, O wayward generation, every one of you would have followed the example of this youth (referring to Anís pressed to His breast), who stood in rank above most of you, and willingly would have sacrificed himself in My path. The day will come when you will have recognized Me; that day I shall have ceased to be with you.'

The second regiment did the dastardly deed. It was high noon on 9 July 1850. The Báb was thirty-one years old.

But this was not the end of the signs and wonders to accompany that fateful day. A great wind suddenly arose, and, gaining in strength, formed itself into a swirling tower of dust. The light of the sun seemed to disappear, and the eyes of the people were blinded. An eerie darkness enveloped the whole city from noon until nightfall. A feeling of doom was everywhere. Shortly thereafter, earthquakes tumbled cities to the ground, sending the peoples fleeing in terror. They knew the wrath of God was upon them.

Nor were the guilty priests and officials to escape punishment for their shameful deeds. Remember the Grand Vizier who first ordered the Báb thrown into prison? He was stripped of everything he had, driven from his own land and died in misery. Remember the bloodthirsty priest who beat the blessed feet of the Báb with his own hand? He awoke one day to find himself completely paralysed, and died a broken man shortly thereafter. Remember the crazed priest of Barfurush who persecuted the defenders of Fort Ṭabarsí? He caught a rare disease that gave him a thirst he could not satisfy no matter how much water he drank, and made him feel cold no matter how much heat he applied to his body. Remember the second Grand Vizier who caused the deaths of the Seven Martyrs, Vaḥíd, Ḥujjat and the Báb? The Shah ordered that he be put to death; his veins were sliced open and he slowly bled to death. Remember the fiendish governor who sent the heads of Vaḥíd and his companions to the Prince? All of a sudden he could not speak, and he never uttered a single word until his last day, when, raising up from his deathbed, he whispered three times, 'Followers of the Báb!', 'Followers of the Bab!', 'Followers of the Bab!' and then fell back dead. Remember the fanatic governor who hounded down all the innocent Bábís? Wild tribesmen captured him, tortured him, disgraced his family before his eyes and then killed him. Remember the second regiment that was marched in and riddled the blessed body of the Báb with their bullets? Soon after, some were crushed to death in an earthquake, and the rest were shot for mutiny. Remember the masses of people who either opposed or were indifferent to the Cause of the Báb? Misery, famine, plague and starvation stalked the land. None escaped the wrath and judgement of God.

On the evening of the martyrdom of the Báb the precious remains of the Báb and his companion Anís were taken down from where they had been suspended. Observers were amazed to see how the two bodies had been blended into one by the hail of bullets. Even more remarkable was the fact that the blessed face of the Báb was unmarked. After dark, the remains were taken to the edge of the city and thrown into a moat. The authorities, fearing the Bábís would preserve and venerate the sacred remains, ordered that soldiers guard over them to prevent any Bábís from taking them away.

A prominent man in the province, named Ḥájí Sulaymán Khán, was a staunch disciple of the Báb. He had arrived in Tabriz intending to rescue Him from His oppressors, but he arrived one day too late – the evil deed had been done. He was a good friend of the mayor of Tabriz, so he went to him to seek his help in recovering the mingled bodies of the Báb and Anís from the moat. The mayor knew of a daring, rough and ready man just right for such a risky task; his name was Ḥájí Alláh-Yár. And ready he was! Quiet as a cat, that very night he was able to steal away the sacred remains right from under the noses of the guards as they slept! He took them straight to Ḥájí Sulayman Khán. The next morning the guards excused themselves, explaining to the authorities that wild beasts had eaten the remains during the night.

Ḥájí Alláh-Yár must have been aware of the sacred nature of his mission, for he refused to accept any reward for his daring deed. Ḥájí Sulayman Khán arranged that the precious remains be put into a wooden chest by a trusted believer and hidden away. Eventually, under the direction of Bahá'u'lláh, these holy relics were secretly carried from place to place, and from land to land until the day came when 'Abdu'l-Bahá, the son of Bahá'u'lláh, laid them to rest in the Shrine constructed for them by Him on Mount Carmel in the Holy Land. Today that sacred dust marks the central point from which radiate the spiritual forces that animate the metropolis of a world-embracing Faith, and beyond, to the rest of the globe.

As for Ḥájí Sulaymán Khán, sometime later, in Tehran, he was to give his life for the Cause of the Báb in such a gruesome manner that it defies the imagination. You, dear reader, may read of his martyrdom in the book by Shoghi Effendi, *God Passes By* (p. 76), which recounts his glorious end when he 'gave evidence to the unquenchable love which the Báb kindled in the breasts of His disciples', earning him a place within the pantheon of the Heroes of the New Age.

And now the story of the Báb has been told. Thinking back, might not the distant voices of the Heroes call to our inner ear? Might not we imagine their calls ringing in our minds? The voices of Quddús, Mullá Ḥusayn, and their companions call, 'Mount your steeds, O heroes of God!' Echoing in turn, the united voices of the Seven Martyrs' cry, 'We shall never deny our Faith!' Rising from the valiant Vaḥíd and his companions comes the call, 'God is most great!' Sounding in return, the voices of the fiery Ḥujjat and his companions' shout, 'O Lord of the age!' Then, over them all, we might hear the blessed voice of the Báb whisper, 'Their blood has been shed in My path. Sweeter indeed is this to me than all else, that its light may endure forever.'

And so, we are touched to our very souls and bow our heads in gratitude that these Heroes of God sacrificed their lives as martyrs to so great a Cause; and that through their sacrifice that Cause would expand and develop, and its purifying light penetrate the most remote regions of the earth, and conquer the hearts of men. Even that you and I are here to tell about it.

THE END

BIBLIOGRAPHY

'Abdu'l-Bahá. *A Traveler's Narrative Written to Illustrate the Episode of the Báb* (1891). Trans. E. G. Browne. Wilmette, IL: Bahá'í Publishing Trust, rev. ed. 1980.

— *Memorials of the Faithful.* Trans. M. Gail. Wilmette, IL: Bahá'í Publishing Trust, 1971.

— *Some Answered Questions* (1908). Comp. L. Clifford Barney. Haifa: Bahá'í World Centre, rev. ed. 2014.

The Bahá'í World: An International Record. Vol. XVIII (1979–1983). Haifa: Bahá'í World Centre, 1986.

Bahá'í World Faith: Selected Writings of Bahá'u'lláh and 'Abdu'l-Bahá. Wilmette, IL: Bahá'í Publishing Trust, rev. ed. 1956.

Bahá'u'lláh. *The Hidden Words of Bahá'u'lláh.* Trans. Shoghi Effendi. Wilmette, IL: Bahá'í Publishing Trust, 1970.

— *Tablets of Bahá'u'lláh Revealed after the Kitáb-i-Aqdas.* Comp. Research Department of the Universal House of Justice. Haifa: Bahá'í World Centre, 1978.

Bahíyyih Khánum: The Greatest Holy Leaf. Comp. Research Department of the Universal House of Justice. Haifa: Bahá'í World Centre, 1982.

Balyuzi, H. M. *The Báb: The Herald of the Day of Days.* Oxford: George Ronald, 1973.

— *Bahá'u'lláh, the King of Glory.* Oxford: George Ronald, 2nd ed. 1991.

— *Muḥammad and the Course of Islám.* Oxford: George Ronald, 1976.

Blomfield, Lady. *The Chosen Highway*. London: Bahá'í Publishing Trust, 1940. RP Oxford: George Ronald, 2007.

Faizi, A. Q. *The Prince of Martyrs*. Oxford: George Ronald, 1977.

Gibbon, Edward. *The Decline and Fall of the Roman Empire*. Vol. V. London: Collier and Son, 1901.

Ḥaydar-'Alí, Ḥájí Mírzá. *Stories from the Delight of Hearts: The Memoirs of Ḥájí Mírzá Ḥaydar-'Alí*. (Originally published as *Bihjatu's-Ṣudúr*, Bombay, 1913.) Trans. and abridged A.Q. Faizi. Los Angeles: Kalimát Press, 1980.

Momen, Moojan (ed.). *The Bábi and Bahá'í Religions, 1844–1944: Some Contemporary Western Accounts*. Oxford: George Ronald, 1981.

— (ed.). *Selections from the Writings of E. G. Browne on the Bábí and the Bahá'í Religions*. Oxford: George Ronald, 1987.

al-Mufid, Shaykh. *Kitab Al Irshad (The Book of Guidance)*. The Muhammad Trust, 1981.

Nabíl-i-A'ẓam (Muḥammad-i-Zarandi). *The Dawn-Breakers: Nabíl's Narrative of the Early Days of the Bahá'í Revelation*. Trans. Shoghi Effendi. New York: Bahá'í Publishing Committee, 1932.

Nicolas, A.-L.-M. *Seyyèd Ali Mohammed dit le Báb*. Paris: Dujarric, 1905.

Shoghi Effendi. *Citadel of Faith: Messages to America, 1947–1957*. Wilmette, IL: Bahá'í Publishing Trust, 1965.

— *Directives from the Guardian*. New Delhi: Bahá'í Publishing Trust, 1973.

— *God Passes By* (1944). Wilmette, IL: Bahá'í Publishing Trust, rev. ed. 1974.

QUESTIONS

Chapters 1 and 2

1. Why, in your opinion, are light and darkness often used to symbolize good and evil?
2. How would you explain the fact that Mullá Ḥusayn was so determined to find the new Messenger?
3. What could be the relationship between Mullá Ḥusayn's determination to seek the Promised One and the fact that the Báb had chosen him to be the first to believe?
4. What could be the reason that Mullá Ḥusayn did not immediately recognize the Báb as the One whom he was seeking?
5. What accounts for the fact that Quddús and Ṭáhirih believed in the Báb without benefit of meeting Him beforehand?
6. What do you see in common between Mullá Ḥusayn, Quddús and Ṭáhirih?
7. The importance of the first believer of a Prophet of God is explained in *Tablets of Bahá'u'lláh*, pp. 184–5. How can the idea that the first believer returns at the beginning of each new Revelation be understood or explained?
8. Do you think the mission given by the Báb to the Letters of the Living was different from that given the ordinary followers of His Faith? Give an explanation for your answer.

Chapter 3

1. What could the charters of liberty in 'Abdu'l-Vahháb's dream symbolize? You can read this story in *The Dawn-Breakers*, pp. 87–90.

2. What happened to Mullá 'Alí; why does he deserve special honour?

3. What could be the reason that the Báb wished to write down the names of the new believers?

4. Discussion: Why would Bahá'u'lláh link straying from justice with failure to recognize the divine origin of the words of the Báb? What indicates that Mullá Ḥusayn understood to some degree the station of Bahá'u'lláh at that time? (see *The Dawn-Breakers*, p. 107)

5. What was one indication that the Cause of the Báb would continue on regardless of what happened to Him?

6. Why was it important that the Báb travelled to the city of Mecca to proclaim His Cause?

7. Discuss and reflect upon the Báb's answer to the warning of the holy men who appeared to Him in a vision while on the road from Mecca.

8. The Báb told Quddús he should be happy to suffer for the Cause of God. Why is this so?

9. How could the manner in which Mullá Ṣádiq demonstrated his belief be emulated by believers today? (One may read an account in an English newspaper of the punishment of Mullá Ṣádiq and Quddús, in Balyuzi, *The Báb*, pp. 77–8)

10. Why can the Prophet change the customs of religion if He wishes? Discuss and reflect upon the reaction of the

followers of old religious customs to such change.

11. Why was Ḥujjat so upset with the student he had sent to investigate the claim of the Báb?

12. Discussion: 'Abdu'l-Bahá's explanation (*Bahá'í World Faith*, pp. 364–5) of a person who is instantly attracted to the Word of God, as were Ḥujjat and Mullá Ṣádiq.

Chapter 4

1. Look up in a history book the story of how Alexander the Great tamed the great horse Bucephalus, and compare it with how the Báb tamed the fierce horse. Also, read in the Bible *Isaiah* 1: 2–3.

2. Why did Dayyán convert to the Faith of the Báb?

3. Why did the minister of the Shah want to make the Báb look foolish? How did the trial turn out?

4. What obligation did the Covenant of the Báb impose upon His followers?

5. What was the purpose of the Conference of Badasht?

6. What was the result of the conference?

7. List four important accomplishments in the religion of the Báb described in Chapters 2, 3 and 4.

Chapter 5

1. Discuss and reflect upon the motives of the head priest of Barfurush in his dealings with the Bábís.

2. What brought Mullá Ḥusayn to the town of Barfurush?

3. What could be the reason that the head priest had so much control over the people? Why could they so easily be deceived by their priest?

4. Why did Mullá Ḥusayn give the townspeople so many opportunities to make peace?

5. What did Mullá Ḥusayn mean when he told his companions they were approaching their Karbila?

6. What was the mission of the Imam Husayn, grandson of the Prophet Muhammad? Research Bahá'u'lláh's elucidation of the martyrdom of the Imam Husayn and its meaning in Balyuzi, *Bahá'u'lláh, the King of Glory*, pp. 126–9 and 225–6; a more detailed account of the life of the Imam Husayn can be found in Faizi, *The Prince of Martyrs*.

7. What was Hurr sent to do?

8. How could the Imam Husayn and his party have gone free?

9. What made Hurr go over to the side of Husayn?

10. Do people today, in some way, have to make the same kind of choice that confronted Hurr?

11. Research 'Abdu'l-Bahá's explanation of blasphemy against the Holy Spirit in *Some Answered Questions*, no. 31, pp. 143–5, in connection with the Governor of Kufah striking the mouth of the Imam Husayn.

12. What was the meaning of the dream of the keeper of the Shrine of Shaykh Ṭabarsí?

13. How was the mistaken attack upon the village corrected?

14. How did the Bábís change the tomb of Shaykh Ṭabarsí?

15. What were Bahá'u'lláh's instructions to Mullá Ḥusayn?

16. To understand the reason for Quddús's greatness, read *Some Answered Questions*, no. 11, pp. 62–3, *A Traveler's Narrative*, pp.18–19, and *The Dawn-Breakers*, pp. 263–5. What did Mullá Ḥusayn recognize in Quddús?

17. Why did the Shah send an army against the Bábís?

18. Name the four events that fulfilled the dream of the keeper of the Shrine.

19. Why do you think Mullá Ḥusayn was so fearless when facing death? Research Bahá'u'lláh's answer to this question in *The Bahá'í World*, Vol. XVIII, p. 11, selection VI.

20. What were the last words of Quddús?

21. Further reading: a short biography of Quddús in *The Dawn-Breakers*, pp. 414–15, and of a survivor of the upheaval, Hand of the Cause of God Ismu'lláhu'l-Aṣdaq, in *Memorials of the Faithful*, pp. 5–8.

22. Research: The comparison made by the Greatest Holy Leaf of the martyrs of Karbila to the Bahá'í martyrs of Yazd at the beginning of the 20th century, in *Bahíyyih Khánum: The Greatest Holy Leaf*, pp. 105–7.

23. Further reading: the meeting between Ḥájí Mírzá Ḥaydar-'Alí and the man who claimed to have shot Mullá Ḥusayn, in *The Delight of Hearts*, pp. 13–14.

Chapter 6

1. Research the explanation by Shoghi Effendi of the significance of the remains of the Prophet in *Directives from the Guardian*, p. 38 (section on 'Manifestation').

2. What was the reason for the hatred of the Grand Vizier for the Bábís?

3. How could those who were arrested have gained their freedom?

4. What could explain why seven of the men made this choice?

5. What was the reason given by the uncle of the Báb for not denying his faith?

6. What was Qurbán-'Alí's explanation of the difference between himself and the Báb?

7. Why did Qurbán-'Alí fling himself upon the fallen uncle of the Báb?

8. What were the final words of Ḥájí Mullá Ismá'íl-i-Qumí? and how might the title given him by Bahá'u'lláh, 'Mystery of Being', be reflected in the manner of his death?

9. Why will the memory of the Seven Martyrs of Tehran not be forgotten?

10. Research the astounding account of the seven martyrs of Tehran of the present day, so closely paralleling those of this chapter, in *The Bahá'í World*, Vol. XVIII, p. 261.

Chapter 7

1. What could be the reason that Vaḥíd determined to spend his last ounce of energy spreading the Cause of the Báb?

2. What, from Ṭáhirih's remark to Vaḥíd, was her feeling about the conversation between him and Bahá'u'lláh?

3. Why did some people oppose the message of Vaḥíd to them?

4. Muḥammad-'Abdu'lláh was ready to take the fight to the enemy, but Vaḥíd advised him not to do so. Muḥammad-'Abdu'lláh did not want to be compared to those who had failed to help the Imam Husayn in a similar situation long ago, so he went on the attack. It appears that many Bábís had a similar attitude about defending their Faith. Research: 'Abdu'l-Bahá's explanation of this attitude in *A Traveler's Narrative*, pp. 22 and 39, and a story of one Bábí's education in this regard, pp. 40–41.

5. What was the result of Muḥammad-'Abdu'lláh's disregard of Vaḥíd's advice?

6. Read in the New Testament, Matt. 13: 45–6, about the pearl of great price. How might these verses apply to Vaḥíd and the revelation of the Báb?

7. Discussion and reflection: the people of that day were accustomed to following a strong leader, as evidenced by the events in this drama. How does this apply today?

8. Compare the fighting qualities of the Bábís and their enemy, and try to contrast the motives which prompted a common soldier in the service of the government with those of a Bábí defender.

9. How did the governor finally overcome Vaḥíd and his companions?

10. What are the similarities between the martyrdoms of the Imam Husayn and Vaḥíd?

11. What effect can the sacrifice of Vaḥíd and his fellow Bábís have on us who read of it today?

Chapter 8

1. Why did the priests want to destroy Ḥujjat?

2. Before he became a Bábí, what was Ḥujjat's goal in his religion?

3. What was, in your opinion, the difference between the thinking of Ḥujjat and the priests about the purpose of religion?

4. How did the Tablet to Ḥujjat from the Báb dramatically change everything?

5. What can we understand about some aspects of life after

death from the answer of the Báb to Ḥujjat's offer to come and rescue Him?

6. What was the difference between the reasons of the priests and the Grand Vizier for opposing Ḥujjat?

7. What events led to open conflict between the Bábís and their enemies?

8. Why is Shaykh Muḥammad-i-Túb-Chí so worthy of being remembered?

9. Research: to further understand the statement of Ḥujjat that 'God has decreed that in every age the blood of the believers is to be the oil of the lamp of religion', read Shoghi Effendi's elucidation of this theme in *The Bahá'í World*, vol. XVIII, section vii, p. 37. Discuss the ramifications of the difference between this attitude toward martyrdom and the belief of many people that sacrifice for religious reasons is a needless waste.

10. How could one explain the great difference in the conduct of the enemy in their camp and that of the Bábís in the fort?

11. Research: study the history of Joan of Arc, seeking to find parallels between her and Zaynab.

12. What could account for the warrior spirit that so filled Zaynab?

13. What were the vital contributions of the Bábí women in the resistance?

14. Why were the young Bábí bridegrooms willing to leave their brides and give their earthly lives in defence of the Cause of the Báb?

15. Name two virtues of the eldest of the five Bábí brothers.

16. Why did Ḥujjat agree to the peace offer of the general when he knew it was a trick?

17. Ḥujjat gave his followers a hard choice when he encouraged them to escape with their lives and leave him to his fate. Discussion and reflection: what is the difference in the quality of belief between those who stayed and those who followed his advice?
18. Why does it seem that the title conferred upon Ḥujjat (The Proof) by the Báb is so wonderful?
19. What new name was given by the Báb to the city of Zanján?

Chapter 9

1. How might one account for the fact that every effort to destroy the Cause of the Báb only caused it to grow stronger?
2. Research: 'Abdu'l-Bahá's discussion on the subject of interference in matters of conscience, in *A Traveler's Narrative*, p. 40. Why is persecution for matters of belief a blessing in disguise?
3. What was the reply of the Grand Vizier to the protest that it would not be right to put a descendant of the Prophet Muhammad, which the Báb was, to death? How is this reason to execute the Báb different from that of the priests?
4. What was the meaning of the Tablet of the Báb to Bahá'u'lláh?
5. What may have been the Báb's reason for His statement that He would prefer to be slain by one of His followers rather than by the hand of the enemy? What did Anís's response to this statement demonstrate?
6. Why did the execution of the Báb fail the first time?
7. How might one explain the awful end that came to most

of those who persecuted the Báb and His followers?

8. Research: the significance of the resting place of the remains of the Báb, as explained by Shoghi Effendi; see 'The Center of Nine Concentric Circles', in *Citadel of Faith*, pp. 95–6.

9. Research: summarize each of the eight paragraphs of the eulogy written by Shoghi Effendi on the occasion of the commemoration of the Centenary of the Martyrdom of the Báb, in *Citadel of Faith*, pp. 80–83.